The Bharathi I Knew

The Bharathi I Knew

M.K. Yadhugiri Ammal

Translated by
Premila Paul and Subash Jeyan

Vitasta

TAMIL NADU TEXTBOOK AND EDUCATIONAL SERVICES CORPORATION
LEARN THOROUGHLY

Published by
Renu Kaul Verma
Vitasta Publishing Pvt Ltd
4348/4C, Ansari Road, Daryaganj
New Delhi - 110 002
info@vitastapublishing.com

ISBN 978-81-960413-3-5

First published in Tamil in 1954

English translation

First Edition 2023
First Reprint 2025
MRP ₹ 450

Edited by Anuradha Mukherjee
Cover & Layout by Somesh Kumar Mishra
Printed by Chaman Enterprises, Delhi

MISSION STATEMENT

This is an initiative of the Tamil Nadu Textbook and Educational Services Corporation (TNTB & ESC) under the aegis of one of the announcements for the year 2021-22, by Honourable Minister for School Education Thiru. Anbil Mahesh Poyyamozhi to identify and translate into English, Kannada, Malayalam and Telugu, Tamil literary works, that they might enhance the reach of Tamil antiquity, tradition and contemporaneity and enrich World literature and to also translate significant literary voices from other Dravidian languages into Tamil. Both ventures are to be undertaken as either independent or joint publications with collaborating publishers.

Members, Academic Advisory Committee (Translation)

1. Dr. R. Balakrishnan, IAS, Researcher and Writer
2. Thiru. S. Ramakrishnan, Writer
3. Thiru. S. Madasamy, Educationist

Project Execution Team

1. Thiru. Dindigul I. Leoni, Chairperson, TNTB & ESC
2. Dr. M. Aarthi. IAS, Managing Director, TNTB & ESC
3. Dr. C. Usha Rani, Member Secretary, TNTB & ESC
4. Dr. T. S. Saravanan, Honorary Advisor (Translations), TNTB & ESC
5. Dr. P. Saravanan, Assistant Director (Publications), TNTB & ESC
6. Thiru. M. Appanasamy, Consultant, TNTB & ESC
7. Tmt. Mini Krishnan, Co-ordinating Editor, TNTB & ESC

The publisher has no objection to this English translation being used to facilitate transfers into other languages.

Dedication

I offer this book as a small token of love to
my father and Bharathi's close friend
Sri Srinivasaachariyar

Yadhugiri

The translators dedicate this book to

Paul L. Love and R. Padmanabhan Nair
Teachers extraordinaire

Contents

Translators' Note

Subramania Bharathi (1882-1921), as it happens with all great and nationalist poets who fought for Indian Independence, has been appropriated by the narrative of Tamil and Indian nationalism. And with the passage of time, he has become larger than life, a secular holy figure if you will, in some ways frozen and beyond criticism. In innumerable ways, Bharathi became Bharathiyar.

That is in the nature of nationalist narratives, it needs heroes to prop up against colonial narratives. But by idealising/ idolising a person, by making him/her fit into a larger narrative, one sometimes loses a sense of the actual person, the life s/he led with all that went into making that person unique.

It is, therefore, refreshing to read M.K. Yadhugiri Ammal's account of Bharathi's life in Pondicherry between the years 1912 and 1918. She, no doubt, admired him and his poetry but that doesn't stop her from portraying Bharathi as she saw him, including his experiments with drugs in an effort to find 'new words'. She could write, for example, without hesitation the following about Bharathi: "The songs Bharathiyar sang about women's freedom were only that, just words. He made Chellamma do whatever he wanted. Chellamma could rarely follow her own desires." It humanises Bharathi, brings him back into the sphere of the every-day, with all its contradictions, dilemmas, and bunglings. And in the process, puts in perspective the real magnitude of his poetry.

Yadhugiri Ammal writes in simple, everyday conversational Tamil, not the register of scholarly or literary Tamil in vogue in the first half of the twentieth century. We hope that we have managed to preserve in another language one woman's love and admiration for Bharathi the poet and the person.

We would like to acknowledge our debt to Mini Krishnan for her tireless and pioneering work in the field of translation and express our sincere thanks to the Tamil Nadu Textbook Corporation (TNTB) for bringing out this book as a part of its translation project.

Premila Paul
Subash Jeyan

Introduction

Introducing Srimathi Yadhugiri Ammal and her book *Bharathi Ninaivugal* (*The Bharathi I Knew*) gives rise to two contradictory feelings in my mind. On the one hand, I am delighted that a book that had been lying idle for fifteen years for want of a publisher is finally getting published. On the other hand, I am sad that the author, who was with us until recently, is no more, at a time when her greatest desire was getting fulfilled. Srimathi Yadhuguri Ammal was a completely satisfied woman when she passed away on August 2, 1954. She had made all the arrangements for the release of the book on Bharathi Remembrance Day. She had been quite ill for years and it seemed as if she had been waiting only to complete the preparations for the final printing of the book.

Bharathiyar, who came to Chennai in 1904 as the assistant editor of *Swadesamitran*, became the editor of *India*, the vibrant Tamil weekly, within just two years. *India* was the resounding voice of a youth organisation called Chennai Jana Sangam.

Bharathi, Va.Ve.Su. Iyer, Mandayam Srinivasaachari, and S. Duraisamy Iyer were some of the prominent members of this organisation whose members considered Bal Gangadhar Tilak as their leader. It was the Mandayam family who financed and managed the magazine. The fiery essays, the editorials that asked tough questions, and the cartoons published in *India* that made fun of the Britishers and their Indian cronies caused our invaders to hang their heads in shame. It created a big revolution in Tamil Nadu politics.

In 1908, people were apprehensive that Bharathiyar might get arrested. One day, the police came to the *India* magazine office with a warrant to arrest its editor. Bharathiyar managed to escape because legally, he was not its registered editor. The official editor of *India*, M. Srinivasan, was arrested and punished instead.

After that incident, an arrest warrant for Bharathiyar was expected any day. Some young political activists got together, discussed the situation and decided that rather than being in Chennai and risking arrest, it was better for Bharathiyar to go to Puducherry and work for India's freedom from there.

Accordingly, Bharathiyar managed to hoodwink the police and escaped to Puduvai. A few weeks later, Mandayam Srinivasaachariyar also reached Puduvai. The *India* press also followed suit soon after. After hibernating for a few weeks, the magazine soon made its presence felt with renewed energy.

Bharathiyar showed that it was possible for Indian freedom fighters, those who were not welcome in British India, to work effectively for Indian freedom from French India. Two great political leaders, Aurobindo Ghosh and Va.Ve.Su. Iyer, soon followed the same path.

It was not surprising that the unity and cooperation among freedom fighters who sought refuge in Puduvai spread to their families as well. Srinivasaachariyar's family provided solid support for Bharathiyar's family and vice versa. After Va.Ve. Su. Iyer's arrival in Puduvai, the families of Bharathiyar and Aachariyar found renewed support in Iyer's family.

While describing their lives during that time, Va.Ve.Su. Iyer's wife Srimathi Bhagyalakshmi Ammal said, 'After getting acquainted with Bharathi's wife Chellammal, the families of Bharathi, Srinivasaachariyar, and Iyer mingled with one another as one family. We would go to the beach together almost every day. Inspired by the sea and the sky, Bharathi would forget himself and start singing'.

Srimathi Yadhugiri Ammal, the author of *Bharathi Ninaivugal* (*The Bharathi I Knew*), is Mandayam Sri Srinivasaachariyar's eldest daughter. She was a young girl when Bharathiyar was in Puduvai. She was very close to Bharathiyar for quite a number of years and was privileged to be the recipient of his love and affection. She has described Bharathiyar the poet the way she saw him as a young child.

Bharathiyar's friend in politics, V.O.C, his literary disciples Va. Ra. and Bharathidasan, his wife Chellammal, and daughter Thangammal have all described Bharathi from their individual perspectives. But Srimathi Yadhugiri Ammal paints a portrait of Bharathiyar as a head of a family and as a person from the point of view of a young girl who was much-loved by Bharathiyar. The everyday language of domesticity that she uses lends a unique flavour to the book.

The greatness of a genius can be compared to the splendour of a diamond. It is difficult for a single person to see or experience, from just one angle, the total impact of the thousands of rays of light the diamond emits.

It is natural for each person to experience the light from her/his own angle and praise its particular radiance. Sometimes, people claim that only their perception is the right one—the absolute truth. What they have seen is also probably true. But, isn't it possible that a totally different perception of the same diamond by another person, from a different angle, can also be true?

For a comprehensive understanding of the greatness of a genius, it is important to combine the perspectives of different people and their multiple descriptions, to view them all together as a whole. It is only from such a total, comprehensive picture that one can discern the truth. Srimathi Yadhugiri Ammal compiled many rare details of Bharathiyar's life in Puduvai from 1912 to 1918. This book definitely makes its own contribution towards the writing of Bharathiyar's comprehensive biography.

Unfortunately, we have lost the author of this book. But, luckily, Mandayam Sri Srinivasaachariyar, who was Bharathiyar's friend and the editor of his magazine, is still alive. This great leader lives in Delhi with his son.

Another friend of Bharathi, Sri Parali Su. Nellaiyappar, also lives amidst us. I feel it is the foremost duty of those who admire Bharathi to record the firsthand accounts of these two great men and that of Sri S. Duraisami Iyer and publish them as a book for the benefit of the Tamil people.

If we can thus publish the many different details and events of Bharathi's life from multiple perspectives, the publication of a comprehensive biography of Bharathi is not far away.

Chennai
3/9/1954

R.A. Padmanabhan
Journalist and Historian

Foreword

In this world, a man's first and greatest love is reserved for his children and then for his *shishyas.* His instinctive love for them is boundless.

I feel proud now to acknowledge that I had the good fortune to be both Bharathiyar's *shishya* and favourite daughter about forty years ago in Puducherry.

In the Puducherry of that time, freedom fighters were called *swadeshis.* Some of them chose to and some were forced to live as exiles in Puducherry because of their commitment to the cause of Indian Independence. Prominent among them were Mahakavi Bharathiyar, Sri Va.Ve.Su. Iyer, Sri Aurobindo Ghosh, my father Sri Srinivasaachariyar (who managed Bharathiyar's weekly, *India*), and Sri Thirumalaachariyar. Many other freedom fighters, too, used to drift in and out of Puduvai.

My father and Bharathiyar used to be close friends even during their days in Chennai. Our families were also close to each other and Bharathiyar used to visit our house frequently. Whenever he finished composing a song or a poem, he used to take delight in singing it for us.

There was no fixed time for Bharathiyar's visits to our house. He would come whenever he felt like it. Sometimes, during such visits, I would be learning my lessons or singing the religious hymns taught to me by my mother. But the moment Bharathiyar arrived, my attention would get diverted upstairs, where he would be singing a newly composed song to my father. I would try to imitate him and sing the first stanza of that song just like him. If Bharathiyar happened to notice it, he would call me upstairs and give me the paper on which he had scribbled down the song.

I did not feel particularly fortunate on such occasions. I used to keep all those papers Bharathiyar gave me in a book. Unfortunately, that book was trapped under a wall and was destroyed during the cyclone that devastated Puduvai on 22 November 1916.

Since I was quite young when I had these interactions with Bharathiyar, I did not have the capacity to absorb the profound ideas in his conversations. When I recollect them now, I can see rare and significant truths in each of his words and statements. I think the world should also know about them.

The moment Bharathiyar came to our house, I used to give him a vessel of water, betel leaves, and areca nuts as my offerings, without fail. Sometimes Sri Va.Ve.Su. Iyer also used to accompany him. But Iyer would come mostly in the evenings, now and then in the mornings, but not at other times.

Though there were many *shishyas*, friends, relatives and many in the general public who were aware of Bharathiyar's greatness and wished him success, they could not create conditions in which he could focus on writing poetry without other worries. But, Bharathiyar himself, amidst all the troubles in the world, never failed to be keenly aware of and appreciate the joys of nature. His days were spent singing and talking happily to friends.

Bharathiyar was a committed social reformer. He used

to say, 'The Tamil world is still in an infant stage. It has just opened its eyes and has started crawling. It is yet to gain the power to look around and observe the world keenly'.

Bharathiyar had little patience with certain traditional social practices and wanted to root them out completely. In this respect, Srimathi Chellamma had a slightly different opinion. Chellamma would be cooking in the kitchen following certain customs to avoid pollution. Bharathiyar would enter the house, wash his hands and feet, go straight to the kitchen and eat whatever was there in the utensils. Chellamma would ask him not to touch anything, but he would ignore it. There would be heated arguments between them. Eventually, Bharathiyar would win and Chellamma would keep quiet.

Bharathiyar would readily accept a person's invitation to partake in meals without taking into account that person's caste. He lived the principles he sang about. His actions were always determined by what he believed in, unfazed by practical difficulties or the objections of others.

When he sang, he did it with great emotional fervour and majesty and those listening would get goosebumps. Some of his songs had autobiographical elements. He had composed songs in a variety of forms, sometimes using folk forms like *kummi*, sometimes using the Hindustani and devotional hymn forms.

Nowadays, many famous professional singers sing his songs in different *raga*s beautifully. But those who have been privileged to hear Bharathiyar sing in person would never be satisfied with any of these contemporary renderings. They lack the majesty and the unique, overwhelming emotional impact of Bharathiyar's singing.

Now, there is no place where Bharathiyar's fame has not spread; no place where his poems are not heard. I wish

Bharathiyar were alive to see all this and I long for his presence. I console myself with the thought that his fame will live on forever even though the *maya* of his body is gone.

Bharathiyar did not get his due in his lifetime. At least now, the people of Tamil Nadu should learn to value and celebrate great poetic geniuses living amidst them and create ideal living conditions for them.

I decided to write this because I wanted to share with others whatever I knew about Bharathiyar. These notes were written in 1938-39, but are appearing in print only now. I am not a college-educated woman like present-day girls. I was educated by my father at home. So, please ignore the errors and inadequacies and accept the essence of the thoughts I have recorded.

Bangalore M. K. Yadhugiri
28/7/1954

The Yeleloe Song

Bharathiyar used to thoroughly enjoy the songs of the snake charmers, *dhobis,* rice pounding women, fishermen, and farmers much more than classical music concerts.

One evening, Srimathi Chellamma, Bharathiyar, and the six children from our families were on the Puducherry beach, chatting and having fun. The fishermen, with the day's catch, were singing their hearts out and towing their boat ashore. Bharathiyar, who was talking to us, started applauding their song.

'It seems strange that you should appreciate their song, which has neither meaning nor tune. We do not understand why,' I said.

Chellamma: Don't you know his nature? If a man carrying a Mariamman idol appears on the street playing the *udukkai,* he forgets himself and dances with abandon. It is evening now. The sound of waves in the background and the rhythm of this meaningless song...you can imagine what these would do to him!

Getting up, Bharathiyar approached the fishermen with a pen and paper. He asked an old man there to repeat that song line by line. He wrote it down, corrected the errors and, coming back to us, said, 'You were all making fun of me; the fishermen actually taught me the fundamental principle of the universe'.

Chellamma: Aha! Everyone is a guru to you, not just the head priest in a mutt.

Bharathi: Look here Chellamma! Do not talk to me about meaningless superstitions. I refuse to believe in practices that are not essential or do not have any truth in them. Even if the fisherman does a menial job, my soul and his soul are the same.

I intervened, 'Why is the discussion suddenly becoming a serious argument? Tell us about the meaning and the beauty of the fisherman's song'.

Bharathiyar began to sing from his notes on the paper. We lost ourselves in his singing and did not notice that half an hour had gone by. I still remember the tune and the effortless singing.

As soon as he finished, my brother Sami asked him, 'You haven't yet told us the meaning of the song. It is getting late, do tell us the meaning before we leave'. We were so immersed in the beauty of the song that we did not realise that it was getting late.

Bharathi: Sami, what was there before the world came into being?

Sami: You cannot answer a question with another question.

Anyway, what do I know?

Bharathi: I am not just a guru; I am a crazy mix of a *shishya* and a guru. If I tell you everything, how will I know the extent of your knowledge?

Me: It is stated in *Naalayira Divya Prabandham* that there existed water before the earth. And, it is said that our God was seated there on a banyan leaf.

Bharathi: Incredible! Is your God different from our God? Are we still not free of this ancient madness?

Me: I am still a small girl. I do not know enough. It is getting late. Tell us the meaning of the song.

I started tugging at his shirt.

Bharathi: In the beginning, the original cosmic principle took the form of a fish in the water. Then it was born as a tortoise and lived as an amphibian on both land and water. Then it became a pig, spending more time on land and less in the water. And then it transformed into a lion…then became half wild animal and half human being. They have beautifully depicted the sense of justice inherent in animal nature in the Yeleloe song. In the city, people keep talking about bharathams, myths, and music concerts. They are kids who do not know how to experience and enjoy life.

Chellamma: Why have you stopped? Go ahead, tell us more.

Bharathi: Now you see the real meaning, but you made fun of me before. Do you like the song now?

Chellamma: I did not have a clue about these stories. I could not understand a word of their song or its meaning.

Bharathi: You will understand if you listen carefully. It seems Maha Vishnu was born a dwarf and then became the original man. When man came into being, laws and rules became necessary. So, he was born as Sri Raman, one who established dharma and lived by it. As these were drab rules that lacked life's essence, he was born as Krishna, to fashion wise and contextual dharmic behaviour. He then demonstrated the world's value system along with Arjuna. Born as Buddha, he revealed the values of non-violence and abstinence. He will be born as Kalki to bring about a fusion of all religions. We will not get to see that; probably our children might. That is the meaning of the song.

Chellamma: What? No mention of Sivan at all?

Me: It was Vishnu who took ten *avatars*. He is the original man.

Bharathi: Whether it is Sivan or Vishnu, all are the same. You call him Sivan; Yadhugiri calls him Vishnu; I say they are all one. It is getting late. Let us go.

Bharathiyar got up. So did we, and our conversation continued on the way back.

This incident happened many years ago. But I can see it in my mind's eye as if it all happened right at this moment.

Breaking Free

One Friday evening, Swaminathan Dikshidar's daughter Meena and I went to Bharathiyar's house on Eswaran Dharmaraja Temple Street. Chellamma was not her usual lively, cheerful self. It was the end of the month…

We chatted among ourselves as usual. Meena went back home at six o'clock. Bharathiyar also had to go out. Chellamma and I were the only ones at home. We remained silent for a while and then I began talking to her.

Me: Chellamma, aren't you well? You do not look your usual self.

Chellamma: Nothing is physically wrong with me, Yadhugiri. But I feel as if a worm is gnawing at my mind. I have to unburden myself by sharing it with someone. But you are only a child. What is the use of telling you all this?

Me: It is alright.... Tell me what is bothering you. I'll tell Bharathiyar that this is no way to treat a woman in the house when he is preaching women's liberation to society.

Chellamma: Ayyo, child! You will not understand. It is the end of the month now. We haven't yet paid the milkman last month's dues. He asked me yesterday and I told him that I would pay him next month. He insisted on the payment, but somehow, I pacified him.

She continued, 'See, Bharathiyar is supposed to send an article to *Swadesamitran* today but he has not sent it yet. How will they give him any money? After his bath, coffee, and the routine betel leaves, I talked to him at length. I even put the paper, pen, and ink bottle on the table, then kept the rice on the open winnowing basket outside and went in to change. But he could not bring himself to write. By the time I came out, he had taken a handful of rice and strewn it in the courtyard and was singing as he watched the sparrows peck at them.

'I came out to collect the rice and found that a quarter of it was gone. I could not control my tears. Seeing this he said, "Chellamma, look at these sparrows! How happy they are! Why can't we be like that? You are constantly arguing with me and I keep yelling at you. These sparrows are teaching us the value of harmony. But, we close our eyes and pay no attention to them. Can we get more stupid than this?"

'I could not bear it anymore and blurted out, "Why are you infuriating me? I wanted to get done with the cooking before the children returned from sister-in-law's (Murugesam Pillai's wife) house, had cleaned the rice and lighted the fire, only to find that you had thrown the rice to the sparrows! It will take ten more minutes to clean the rice again. Who knows how long it will be before you get any money? You have not even begun to write the article. The milkman's demands are humiliating. The housemaid has not turned up for two days. Don't you have to think about all these things? And you want me to be happy like these sparrows. God is blind. He only adds to my responsibilities by giving me children." I went inside and somehow managed to finish cooking.

'When I came out after some time, he was singing the song *Breaking Free* to Sakuntala. The child was jumping with joy. He was totally lost in the joy of singing. The sparrows were pecking at the rice. Thangamma was sitting quietly.

'When everyone is so happy, why should I disturb the peace in the house? So, I too sat down there with them.

'It was noon by the time the singing and dancing got over. "I am hungry. Let's go and eat, appa," said Sakuntala. He, too, settled down to eat without a word.

'Then turning to me, he said, "Chellamma, are you still angry? Look here, I am going to send this poem about the sparrows. You'll receive the payment on the first day of the month. Do not worry."

'He is a good man, devoid of deceit and ill will. It is not a problem if we have enough money. But will the publisher send us money if he does not submit an article on time? That is my only grouse.'

I did not react. What can I say? 'A cover has been sent by post today. What if it is a song or an essay?' I said calmly.

'Well...you are just his kind of person. You will endorse everything he does. But I feel a little relief having shared this with you. That is enough for me,' said that noble woman.

Just then Bharathiyar came back to the house.

Bharathi: Yadhugiri, I composed a new song today. Have you seen it?

Me: No, but Chellamma told me about it. Show it to me.

Bharathiyar took a sheet of paper from the table.

Chellamma: Yadhugiri clings onto and absorbs every syllable that you utter. She does not know any better. I narrated what happened this morning to her. She says, "What if it is a song or an essay?"

Bharathi: Yes, she is very right. You will not like what I am going to tell you now. Whether I am around to see it or not, Yadhugiri, you will certainly live to see how much these songs of mine are appreciated and celebrated by all. Tamil Nadu is like a baby that has not even opened its eyes yet. Even if it has, it is still in its infant stage.

He gave me the paper on which he had written the song and sang it for me once. I had memorised the last line of the first stanza, 'Drinking the light as if it were wine'. But it has been printed with a slight alteration. Bharathiyar probably changed it himself later.

They Call it Bharatha Desam

The *swadeshis* in Puducherry used to go for a bath in the sea every Sunday. We usually started by seven o'clock and returned only by ten. A person called Nagasamy also used to join us, apart from my father, Bharathiyar, Iyer, and Thirumalaachariyar. Nagasamy used to work in the office of *India* weekly, which was edited by Bharathiyar and run by my father. After Iyer's arrival in Puducherry, Nagasamy had begun to stay in his house.[1]

Four or five of us children used to accompany these elders to the sea. Five policemen in plain clothes would follow us a furlong behind. On one such Sunday, we saw a snake charmer showing off his tricks with a snake on Gourla Street.

A servant from a white man's house came out, gave him a quarter *anna* and asked him to leave. 'A quarter *anna* is just enough to buy milk for the snake. Won't you give at least a fistful of rice,

1 When this book was released, Nagasamy was in Puduvai Aurobindo Ashram (Editor).

durai?' asked the snake charmer.

Seeing us approach, the snake charmer started playing his flute again and the snake, too, started dancing. 'Sirs, be generous. I am unable to deal with this cold weather. It has been two days since I had rice and I can hardly see. God will bless you…,' he pleaded.

Our mother had given each one of us a packet of turmeric and a quarter *anna*, saying, 'You should not go empty-handed when you are going for a bath in the ocean'. My brother gave away his quarter *anna* to the snake charmer. When he saw money in my hand too, he pleaded with me, 'Amma, give me yours too. I can buy idlis and eat'.

'No. My mother has asked me to drop it in the ocean,' I said and began to walk away.

I do not know what came over Bharathiyar, who was walking in front of us. He tucked the inner layer of the *veshti* around his waist and gave the outer layer to the snake charmer.

We waited in a corner for the others so we could regroup. Bharathiyar's gesture had shocked us. Giving away a brand new *veshti* bought just the previous day to a beggar did not seem right to me. The snake charmer went away praising Bharathiyar with all his heart, but he was angry with me for not having given him my quarter *anna*.

We all walked quietly on the sand. When we reached the sea, the adults held on to the children protectively and Bharathiyar took my hand. Before taking a bath, I threw the coin into the ocean, smeared myself with turmeric, held on to his hand, and got into the water.

Bharathi: Yadhugiri, why did you throw that coin into the sea?

Me: It seems the ocean is a king and he will get angry if we do not give him a quarter *anna* or a lime before taking bath.

Bharathi: Who told you this?

Me: My mother. She knows everything. My brother gave away the coin to the snake charmer. The ocean may get angry with him. Please hold him tight.

Bharathi: He is holding Iyer's hand. He's not scared. Will you listen to me?

Me: Tell me.

Bharathi: If you had given your quarter *anna* to the beggar, he would have fed his child. Now, this quarter anna will get buried in the sand and it will be of no use to anyone. Isn't it a waste? If you had at least thrown some eatables, the fish would've eaten them. Of what use is a coin to a fish?

Me: What you say is right. It was my mother who told me that. Doesn't she know?

Bharathi: These are meaningless rituals. In the old days, people who took bath in ponds used to throw money in the water so that people who cleaned the ponds could get them. You repeat the practice in the ocean when our elders did it in ponds. Here, the waves do the cleaning and the coin is of no use to them.

Me: We will take the coin back. We'll give it to some beggar on the way home.

Bharathi: Let it go, it's gone. But, don't do it again.

Me: Ok. But you gave away the new *veshti*. What will Chellamma say? Couldn't you have given the torn outer layer?

Bharathi: I have plenty of people who will give me a *veshti*. But who will give him one? Why does it bother you so much? Even I have forgotten about it.

I did not respond.

We went into the sea till the water came up to our chests. The elders lifted up the children and dipped them in the waves. We returned home by 11 o'clock.

There was a water tap in the front courtyard of our house, with a tub always filled to the brim. Bharathi and Ayya[2] had taken a bath there and were changing into new clothes. We had our hot water bath in the backyard, changed our clothes, and went upstairs.

2 Yadhugiri Ammal's father.

Bharathiyar used to call my periappa, father's elder brother, 'Anna'.

Bharathi: Anna, Yadhugiri was upset that I gave away the *veshti* to the snake charmer. Look Yadhugiri, I gave away one *veshti*. To replace that, Ayya has given me two. Tell me who is more generous?

Me: Ok. The tune of the snake charmer's song was very nice. How nice it will be if you can sing to that tune.

Bharathi: I will teach you a song in that tune tomorrow. Now tell me who is the more generous of the two?

Me: Aren't you all the same? Both of you are generous. What I did was wrong. I will not do it again.

Bharathiyar was very happy. He repeated our conversation on the beach to the people present there in English.

The following evening Bharathiyar came to our house and took us all upstairs. He sang *Vande Matharam* first, followed by another,

> *All who hail the land of Bharata*
> *shall overcome*
> *fear's lightning and thunder,*
> *to conquer*
> *their bitterest foes.*
>
> *By Kannan's grace,*

he who triumphed in the Bharata war,
they shall shed their burden of grief,
pick up the sweet weight
of good fortune.

He followed it up with,

By the grace of Bharata's queen
they shall shed their burden of sorrow
and joyfully take on the load
of riches in plenty.

(*Bharatha Desam Enru Peyar Solluvaar*;
Translated from Tamil by Vasantha Surya)

He also sang fourteen stanzas.

I loved to interrupt conversations with questions. I used to do that often with Iyer and Bharathiyar. They, too, would answer my questions patiently.

In that spirit, I raised a question.

'Ok, when will all this materialise? Will we get to see this? Do we need big machines to make needles and nails? Are needles and nails that necessary for a nation? Weapons are very important. You have dismissed it in just one word.'

Bharathiyar said, 'Children raise difficult questions. How can a mother stitch clothes without a needle? Aren't clothes more important than food? Don't you need nails to make boxes, nails to hang photos?'

I did not say anything.

The first four lines in the song above are missing in the books published recently. The last two lines in the first stanza,

By Kannan's grace,
he who triumphed in the Bharata war,
they shall shed their burden of grief,
pick up the sweet weight
of good fortune.

And the two lines that come later,

By the grace of Bharata's queen
they shall shed their burden of sorrow
and joyfully take on the load
of riches in plenty.

are also missing in the books.

Let the Mind be Firm

Kodiyalam Rengasamy Iyengar and R. Rajagopalachari had come to Puduvai after Christmas, in the Tamil month of Thai. They were my father's close friends. During the course of the conversation, Rengasamy Iyengar learnt about Bharathiyar's financial condition.

Because of God's grace, or his fascination for Bharathiyar's poetry, he gave Bharathiyar a gift of a few hundred rupees.

The situation back then was very tense. There were bombings in Delhi. It was a very difficult and trying time for *swadeshis*. As soon as Chellamma received Rengasamy Iyengar's money, she bought a few gold sovereigns, made some jewellery and, with the rest of the money, bought the yearly supply of rice, dhal, tamarind, chillies, etc.

In Puducherry, wages were calculated and given usually for 12 measures/*ser*[3]. By pounding 12 *ser* rice, one could earn a wage of a quarter measure of rice and one measure of broken rice grains. There were no machines to do the job back then. Women would visit homes, pound rice and clean them for use.

One day, a woman was pounding rice in Bharathiyar's house. Bharathiyar had just begun to write a story in English about Annie Besant (I do not remember whether it was 'The Fox with the Golden Tail' or 'The Fox with no Tail'). Chellamma could see that he was not able to concentrate on the story.

Chellamma: I'll ask her to do the job tomorrow.

Bharathi: No. Let her do her job. Why do you stop that?

Chellamma: You sat down to write something. The noise may disturb you.

Bharathi: That sound urges me to seek the blessings of Parasakthi. Do not stop her.

Chellamma: Ask Parasakthi to fill our stomachs first.

Bharathi: You want me to work like a slave? I gave you all that I had. Don't force me anymore.

Chellamma: I will not insist. You said you wanted to publish a book. It is better to do that when you still have some money.

3 Translators' note: In India, the act which established the metric system in 1956 defined the *ser* as exactly 0.93310 kilogramme

Bharathi: Look here, if you keep pestering me, I will leave the house.

Chellamma: If you go away, I too will go my own way. Why take on these problems? Let somebody else bring up the children.

Bharathi: What! Don't I have the ability to take care of my children? Who do you think you are talking to?

Chellamma: Unlike you, I cannot seek Parasakthi's blessings. I can only ask you. What is wrong with that? Why lose your temper over it?

Bharathi: Now that you have talked about the situation, am I incapable of carrying out my responsibility? You bring up the issue of the children unnecessarily. They have done nothing wrong.

Chellamma: I am not saying anything about the children. You said that you will go your own way and I just replied that I, too, can do the same.

Bharathi: Do not provoke me. I know my responsibility. Will you complete the rest of your work?

Chellamma went to attend to her work and Bharathiyar attempted to write something. But he was restless. His attention was drawn to the song of the pounding woman. The way she sang 'hum hum' at the end of each line seemed very inviting and gave him an idea for a song. He took a paper and penned down the lyric of *Manadhil Urudhi Vendum* (Let the Mind be Firm).

He then completed a story as well and sent it to the office for printing.

I happened to go to their house that evening. Chellamma was measuring out the rice. Bharathiyar had just returned home. After inquiring about me, he said, 'I wrote a new song today Yadhugiri!' I requested that he share it with me. 'He seeks Parasakthi's blessings. We seek his blessings,' quipped Chellamma.

Bharathiyar began to sing his song. The lady who was pounding rice was shocked and angry. 'Why do you tease me like this, Sami? We sing so that we are not conscious of the physical strain of work. Why do you make fun of me like that? Isn't that an insult to our profession?' she quarrelled.

'Ayyo *amma*, why do you get angry? Your song was so different from the usual songs of rice-pounding women. This is a magical song, just like yours. Why are you angry? I am not making fun of you at all,' he pacified her.

She was not convinced. 'If children do this, you should reprimand them. But when you yourself do such a thing, what are we to do?'

Chellamma intervened, 'Hey woman, Iyer [Bharathi] is not teasing you. He has composed a poem in the same tune as your song so that it can be preserved for posterity. Do not quarrel like a mad woman. You can take your share of the broken rice and leave if you have finished your job'.

The woman responded, 'How do I know that Iyer was composing a song? Surprising! He sings just like me…how quickly he has made it! I'll leave now, amma'.

Bharathi: I must have got up at an inauspicious hour this morning. I have already quarrelled with two.

Me: Who else did you quarrel with?

Bharathi: Who else? My wife, of course.

Me: Tell me, what is the use of celebrating women's freedom in your poems if you quarrel with your wife at home?

Chellamma: Yadhugiri, ask him if what he did today was right.

Bharathi: You were right. But you should not be so forthcoming every time.

Me: Tell me, what was it about?

Chellamma: If he abdicates family responsibility and goes away, can I not do the same?

Me: Chellamma is also human, just like you. Why can't she also opt out? Isn't that too a matter of personal freedom?

Bharathi: You are yet a child. You will not understand. You have to be tactful in taming a wild bull. If you yank at it hard, it will run away. I can go away anytime I want. But Chellamma cannot. Even if she has the freedom to do so, her responsibility is bigger.

Me: If you speak in puzzles, how will I understand? Explain it to me in detail...

Bharathi: Chellamma, tell her yourself. Maybe it will take the weight off your mind.

Chellamma narrated everything that happened.

Me: Do you mean to say that only you are concerned for the children and not Chellamma?

Bharathi: Both of us have equal responsibility. But she is the one who feeds, I am the one who earns. Between us, there is no need for a hierarchy.

Me: Ok Chellamma, henceforth you can cook only when you feel like it.

Bharathi: No. Any work has to be done sincerely and in the proper way. But it will be good if the man is also sensitive in his behaviour.

Chellamma: I am ignorant and tactless.

Bharathi: Do you know the effect your reprimand had on me this morning? I have already given the story for printing.

Chellamma: I get very angry when a woman talks ill of her husband, and do not like it at all. But when things become unbearable, one feels like complaining, at least to the door if nobody else.

Bharathi: The push you gave in the morning made me complete the work. Shall we go to the beach? Yadhugiri, why don't you join us?

We all got ready to go to the beach. But, I want the whole world to know the words Bharathiyar uttered then.

Bharathiyar: You work so hard in the house and it is a sin to slight you and your work. You bring up the children. You urge us to do our duties for the children at the right time. These are not like old times. If a person is not responsible enough, you must point it out to him. But there must not be any compulsion. What Chellamma said was right. I was blinded by my love for poetry. Two things happened in the heat of the moment. We have lovely children at home, but we are not lucky enough to adorn them with gold ornaments. The penury of poets is a well-known fact from ancient times. Tamil does not have too many monetary rewards for a poet. If a Tamil child celebrates Goddess Lakshmi, they will receive grace and if the woman of the house sees that everything is right at home, the man may live without any worry or disease. He will not go against her words either. What the woman needs the most is money to run the house. If there is money, my Chellamma will rule the world. She admonishes me only because there is no money. She demands it and quarrels with me because of that. Still, she manages with great difficulty to feed me. The world should know this and there should be an end to our difficulties. Only a fool keeps thinking about the past. We should wash away our dirt and troubles, just like we wash our dirty clothes and put them out to dry every day. Like how the sun rises anew every morning, we should enjoy new experiences every day. My Chellamma is the most precious soul! My wealth! She is my all, my everything. She is Bhagyalakshmi!

At least now, the Tamil world should know the pain he experienced. It is an important duty of ours to improve the livelihood prospects of poets like him. If we had spared him such mental agony, he probably would have lived a little longer. But, who can understand God's design?

Three Loves

In Puducherry, a music band performed in front of the Dupleix statue on the beach every Thursday. The musicians performed for almost an hour, standing the whole time, with French children dancing around them. It was a lovely sight.

Bharathiyar did not like crowds. So, he took us away to the seashore. On the way, Thangamma asked, 'Appa, their music sounds strange. They play it at a very high pitch. Will it sound good if we sing like that?'

Bharathi: It is a different kind of music. It jumps from a low pitch to a high pitch in one go. In our music, we move up step by step and move down in a similar way. They sing one note in a low pitch and another in a high pitch.

Thangamma: Will it be nice if we too sing like that? Can we?

Bharathi: If we can do it properly, it will sound nice.

Thangamma: Tomorrow is Saraswathi festival. Will you compose a song on Saraswathi in this style, Appa?

Bharathi: Okay.

The band finished one song and started another.

Me: It will be nice if you sing about Lakshmi too, in this style.

Bharathi: Yadhugiri, as you suggested, I will sing another song on Lakshmi in this style.

Chellamma: People perform Durga puja in Calcutta and Kasi. Our difficulties will end if we sing on Sakthi.

Just then, the band played four lines at a lower octave and four at a higher octave.

Bharathi: Chellamma, what you said is also right. Thangamma wanted a song on Saraswathi. Yadhugiri wanted one on Lakshmi. You have asked for one on Kali. I will sing on all three tomorrow.

Thangamma: How will you sing on all three? In three different tunes?

Bharathi: First on Saraswathi, second on Lakshmi, third on Kali. I will sing on all three in three different *ragas*.

Thangamma: What you have composed so far are in folk tunes such as *Nondi Sindhu*, *Kavadi Sindhu*, and *Ananda Kalippu*. The songs need not be in the same tune.

Bharathi: I will sing for you in whatever tune you want.

Thangamma: We ask because we like this band's music.

The next day was a day of the *moola* star. Some celebrate the Saraswathi festival on the day of the *moola* star and some on *mahanavami*. We celebrate it on *mahanavami*. As a nod to tradition, we had two dolls in the *golu*. Bharathiyar arrived when my sisters and I were singing and performing the *aarthi* and said, 'Yadhugiri, I will sing a new song for your *golu*. Then you can carry on with the rituals'.

We all sat down in a row. As promised the previous day, Bharathiyar sang on all three—Saraswathi, Lakshmi, and Kali. He sang the song that begins with the line '*Pillai Prayathile*' (During Childhood) and titled *Moondru Kaadhal* (Three Loves) in the three *ragas* of *Saraswathi Manohari*, *Sri Raga*, and *Punnagavarali*. We were simply enthralled. Bharathiyar had narrated a little of his life too in this song.

When you Sing of Tamil Nadu

An association in Chennai had advertised prizes for the best poems written about our country—Rs. 300 awarded for the first, Rs. 200 for the second, and Rs. 100 for the third. We all insisted on Bharathiyar sending a poem for this contest and he, too, agreed. He composed the poem *Senthamizh Naadenum Podhinile* (When you Sing of Tamil Nadu) for this competition, and sent the entry within the deadline.

Each letter in the poem deserves a prize of at least a lakh. If not, ten crores for the ten lines, or ten lakhs, or ten thousand, or at least a minimum of ten hundred rupees. But what the association actually sent was a mere hundred rupees, for the third prize. Bharathiyar was least bothered. Va.Ve.Su. Iyer was upset with the judges. 'The songs that bagged the first and second prizes are nowhere as good as even a line in the poem composed by Bharathiyar. Those poems lack the sweetness, musical rhythm, elegance, and meaning of Bharathiyar's song. The difference between them is like that between a mountain and a valley. Those poems are like countless strewn flowers without a unifying thread to string them together,' he complained. He often expressed his sadness that people did not know the intrinsic worth of Bharathiyar.

'This is expected. The association may have already decided to give the prize to somebody else. Giving me the third prize is just a way of fooling the public, that is all. Why are you upset over this? We only have that much luck,' Bharathiyar consoled him.

'We have no one to highlight and showcase the poetry of Bharathiyar like our Peruman did for the *Prabandhams* of Alwars', lamented Iyer.

Iyer was thrilled to see Bharathiyar's poetry get wide circulation after his death. The poem that could get only a third prize is now popular and sung in different tunes whereas there is no trace of the poems that managed to get the first and second prizes.

***

Today, the eldest of my younger brothers died of diarrhoea. He was two years old. None of the medicines worked and his sudden death shattered my father. He had remained strong and determined in very difficult situations such as when a large amount of money was lost in an attempt to get an independent Indian shipping line going, when the magazine *India* was stopped abruptly, or when the government hounded the *swadeshis*. But the death of my brother was a cruel jolt. It weakened him physically. When this tragedy struck, Va.Ve.Su. Iyer and Bharathiyar used to spend the whole day talking or playing chess with him. They would go by four in the evening to Aurobindo Ghosh's house, discuss the Vedas and the Upanishads, and return only by ten or eleven at night.

The day the child died, they returned home by two in the afternoon after the burial. Bharathiyar was deeply disturbed and did not want to eat anything. He prayed to Devi for a blessing. He sang the song *Nalladhor Veenai Seidhey* (When you Make an Exceptional Veenai) for the children in the *Nondi Sindhu* tune, and titled it 'A Request'.

My grief-stricken mother was also afflicted by ailments, including diarrhoea. As she could not be cured by the usual medicines, they wanted to try alternative native medicines. Fearing that her grief would grow more intense if we stayed confined to the house, Chellamma, my sisters, my mother and I would go to a well pump (that was called 'underground Gangai') every morning and have our bath there. On some days, we used to go to the well as early as six in the morning to have an oil bath. Chellamma would insist on taking us to the beach by six in the evening. We would return home by nine. Three months went by like this.

Iyer and my father would pass time playing chess. They would have the squares printed on a thick sheet and play on it. The first letters of the King, Minister, Elephant, Horse, and Soldier would be written on the printed piece of paper. My father suffered frequently from headaches and chest pain. So, Iyer and Bharathiyar were always by his side.

One day, we all went to the Villianur river for a bath. Some festival was being celebrated there. I think it was *Aruthra Darisanam.* A boy named Saminathan accompanied us. We stayed in the house of one of his relatives. The next day, we had a bath in the river, looked around the village and then had our meals.

Around two in the afternoon, we hired a cart and set out with Saminathan. I think Puducherry was three miles away. The cart's wheel broke on the way and we could not find another one. Since Ranganayaki was a child we asked the cart man to carry her and walked back, talking along the way.

Bharathiyar was surprised that even Chellamma walked all the way back. Later, if she ever complained of pain in her legs, he would tease her asking whether she was returning from *Aruthra Darisanam.*

In those days, we never used to stay away from Bharathiyar's family for long. Six months went past in the above routine—underground Gangai in the morning, beach in the evening. In between, everyone became addicted to astronomy. There was a place where a telescope was installed and it was open to all. We spent our time doing such things.

Women's Liberation

In the month of Maasi, we all, both men and women, accompanied Perumal to the beach for a bath. It was a beautiful sight in Puducherry.

That evening, Bharathiyar, accompanied by his daughter Sakuntala, came by around four. My youngest sister Ranganayaki and Sakuntala are of the same age. They started playing together as usual.

Sakuntala: Ranga, what did you eat today in your house?

Ranganayaki: Fried cluster beans, coconut-curd *pachadi*, and sweets.

Sakuntala: What was special about today?

Ranganayaki: We had a bath in the ocean, worshipped Perumal and ate sweets.

Sakuntala: You know what I mean. What festival is it today?

Ranganayaki: I do not know.

Sakuntala: Don't you know? Today is the first day of the month Maasi.

Bharathiyar, who was listening to their conversation, burst out laughing. 'Children come here. Both of you talk beautifully like parrots–one is a golden parrot and the other an iron parrot. Who wants to be which one?'

Sakuntala: Appa, I am the golden parrot and Ranga the iron parrot. Right?

Ranganayaki: I am the golden parrot, you can be the iron parrot.

Sakuntala: No way. It was my father who asked the question, so I am the golden parrot.

Ranganayaki: Come on, Do not start a fight now. Both of us are golden parrots!

Bharathiyar was overjoyed. He carried Ranga over to my father and told him of their conversation. 'I said something insensitive that could have hurt the children. But this child set it right.' After that incident, he always called my younger sister 'golden parrot'.

Ranganayaki: Am I wrong? Aren't we both fair?

Bharathi: You are absolutely right. Both of you are golden parrots.

Ranganayaki: Then why aren't you carrying Sakuntala?

Bharathi: Come, Sakuntala! Ranga has made you also a golden parrot!

Sakuntala: No, I will not come, appa. You come and get me.

Bharathiyar let them both play together as before. I joined them after finishing my lessons. Bharathiyar said, 'Yadhugiri, did you hear about what Thangamma did today?'

Me: What did she do?

Bharathi: After the bath in the sea, I took both of them to a hotel, as it would get too late for cooking. Sakuntala finished eating without a fuss. "After the holy dip in the sea, I will not eat from an unclean table," Thangamma objected. I ordered another set of idlis on a separate plate for her. The hotel boy brought water in a glass tumbler but Thangamma would not touch it. He then brought the water in a brass tumbler. She complained that the water jug had not been cleaned with tamarind and so refused to take it. The hotel boy was fed up. Then he brought water in a silver jug. By then the idli had turned cold. So he brought another set. The people there were all staring at her. I had finished eating and was watching Thangamma's tantrums. I paid the bill, came out and asked her, "Why are you making such a big fuss? Are you an old woman to insist on old practices?" Thangamma retorted, "So what if I am not an old woman? Does it mean that I should eat from used plates and containers? I don't like this. I feel nauseous. He dumped all the used jugs and tumblers in the same basin for cleaning. He put the coffee tumbler used by the leper we saw on the way in the same wash basin. What's the hurry? What if we wait for one more hour to eat? We will not die. This hotel is very unhygienic. My periamma considers even jack fruit peeled by others unclean. She would not have tolerated this. What Chellamma prepares is enough for me. I feel they are right".

Me: Thangamma is not used to a hotel. My mother has asked us not to buy even cashew or cardamom sweets from hotels.

Bharathi: Let the elders do what they want. But, why such restraints for children?

Me: Is it not good to absorb good habits right from childhood?

Bharathi: I will not take Thangamma anywhere hereafter.

Me: Wasn't she right? Where is the need to eat from plates used by leprosy and TB patients and those with open wounds?

Bharathi: You speak like their lawyer. No use arguing with you.

Me: Well, you tell me what is right. Then I will not argue.

Bharathi: The rules by our elders regarding hygiene are right. But it is wrong when we apply these rules on the basis of caste.

If you eat in a TB-afflicted Brahmin's house, it is not considered wrong. But eating from an able-bodied Sudra is considered unclean and wrong.

There was another amusing incident on the train. A young husband, his wife and I, just the three of us, were in a small compartment. The man and I were chatting about the goings-on in the town and then he stepped out to get coffee. The young woman began talking to me, asking me where I lived and so on. The moment the husband appeared, she froze. Then I went out to buy betel leaves and I saw both of them chatting and laughing happily. The moment I re-entered, they shut up again. What kind of behaviour is this? Sheer stupidity. I felt like giving them a big lecture but controlled myself with great difficulty.

Me: Slaves do not have the freedom to speak in front of masters. But she could not control her curiosity and spoke to you in his absence.

Bharathi: She was a perfect slave. I wanted to ask her about it then restrained myself, not wanting to invite unnecessary trouble.

Me: If this slavery is done away with, women too can converse with people freely. Now they are beaten into walking with bent heads, not even looking at what is in front of them on the street.

Bharathi: Yadhugiri, I am going to write a long essay on women's freedom and also compose songs on the subject. You should all throw away old practices.

Me: You don't seem to be liberating women. You are formulating a different set of rules. Where is the freedom here?

Bharathi: You do not know. The old traditions have become irrelevant. Most countries have pulled ahead of us. Our country is lagging behind with regard to women's freedom.

Me: Whatever you may say, this country has stayed stable because of women. You wear *veshtis* made in mills. We wear hand-spun cotton saris. Our customs, festivals, rituals, literature, epics, mythologies, moral stories, and so on, have all been preserved because of us. Do English teachers like you have time for these? If a white man says something, you would ask your mothers if books existed for the texts retained in their memory.

Bharathi: Well done, you have completely internalised Iyer's lecture. Not bad. It is not a shame to lose an argument with children. It is a matter of pride for a guru to lose to a *shishya*, as many have pointed out.

Me: Let it be. Now you compose a song in a new tune for us to perform the *sobanam*.

Bharathi: Today, Thangamma asked for a song to play for the folk dance. You too have asked for a song. I will bring them tomorrow.

The next day, Bharathiyar showed us the newly composed song *Pengal Viduthalai Petra Mahizhchigal* (Happiness over Women's Freedom). He also sang it for us.

In the Sugarcane Plantation

Somebody had given a speech in English on the hardships faced by Indians in the Fiji Islands. A few editors had requested Bharathiyar to translate that as a poem in Tamil.

One evening, my father (Sri Srinivasaachariyar), Iyer, and I had gone to Bharathiyar's house.

Bharathi: Welcome. Why this visit of the trinity?

Iyer: How come you did not visit us for two days?

Bharathi: I have a bad cold. I immediately get it if I take a bath in cold water. But it does not affect me if I bathe in a river, pond, or ocean. Chellamma is not well and the domestic help has not turned up. To add to these, some editors are after me.

Iyer: Walk a distance of 200 to 300 feet before you have a bath in water from the well. Then you will not get cold.

Bharathi: I can instead go to a pool and have a bath, and enjoy the natural beauty on all sides. I do not enjoy watching the bare walls in the bathroom.

Iyer: Yes, it is good to go to the pond, but when you are unable to go out, try my recommendation. What is the matter with the media persons?

Bharathi: Somebody has given a speech on the hardships faced by Hindu labourers in the Fiji Islands. They have asked me to compose a poem on their plight.

Iyer: What are you calling the song? The Fiji Islands will become well known because of your song.

Bharathi: Considering that, I have called it *Karumbu Thottathile* (In the Sugarcane Plantation).

My father said, 'You did the right thing! One of our folk songs has the words "Oh! My Mother India". In my opinion, the word "India" does not fit in with the Tamil metre'.

Bharathiyar sang *In the Sugarcane Plantation* for us. An inconsolable sadness overcame me after listening to it. Bharathiyar tried to cheer me up, saying, 'Crazy girl.... Why are you crying for those living thousands of miles away?'

Iyer: When we adults ourselves are crying, how do you expect a small girl to react? I am not surprised. Have the government officials said that they cannot do anything about it?

Sri Sri: That is why Bharathi has pleaded with the gods to do something about it.

Iyer: This is a sheer atrocity! The action of the agent who tempted our people with promises but treated them mercilessly is condemnable.

Bharathi: You are behind the times. We can only try to prevent more people from getting duped but cannot save those who are already trapped on the island. I read in a paper about an incident—A married man had just had his food and had gone to work. His wife had finished her work and was sitting with her child. There was no one around. A man came to the house and brought a note for her, which stated, "Come immediately, your husband is about to die". She locked the house and went with him without a second thought. That rogue took her to the port, where a ship was about to set sail. "Why did he come to the ship?" she asked him. "His superior officer had sent him on an errand to deliver a letter to the captain of the ship. When he was climbing the ladder on the ship, he felt giddy, fell and hurt his head," the fellow said. The gullible woman trusted him and got onto the ship. Before she could reach the upper deck, the ship set sail. There were many women like her trapped on the ship. When the ship started sailing, they began to cry. When she asked them the reason, they said, "We are now slaves. We have been duped and brought here to sexually satisfy the Indian men already working in Fiji". So many families have been abused and broken like this.

Iyer: What happened to the husband?

Bharathi: There was a note left for him in the window which said, "I cannot lead a life of penury with you. I want bigger things in life. Forget me". He registered a complaint with the police. Where would the police search for a woman who has left the country? That was the end of her story.

Sri Sri: Why can't they tell the truth and hire them? This is wrong. They are getting away with it because there is no one to question them.

Iyer: Not possible. However poor they may be and whatever difficulty they may be in, it is the men who go out to work. They will never send the women out to work, especially to unknown places. There are not enough women among the Indians in the Fiji Islands. So the officials on the island indulge in such atrocities.

Bharathi: If it is just one isolated incident, we can try to do something about it. The problem is much bigger. What is the use of grieving over it?

Me: If all the women pleaded with the captain, wouldn't he take pity on them and let them go?

Bharathi: He is a wily fellow! He traps women from this country and sells them for this evil purpose. If they talk too much, they will be whipped.

Me: What if they all jump into the sea? Are they all treated like this?

Bharathi: No. Some orphans, poor women, and uneducated and ignorant women are all gathered together and sent by sea every three or four months. They get duped by the agents' sugar-coated description of Fiji, which convinces them that life in the Fiji Islands is heaven when it is actually hell on earth.

Sri Sri: Yadhugiri does not have experience with the world. If you divulge any more details, she will be terrified.

Iyer: Children should also get exposed to the wiles of the world. If we protect them from such things, they will find it difficult to cope with reality later on.

Bharathi: No, we should not expose children to evil such as these. If we expose them to all that is good in the world, God will give them the strength to face difficulties.

Iyer: They should be a little daring as well.

Bharathi: Have no fear Yadhugiri. Kali will save them from slavery because of my song. Get me some water from Chellamma. We are all happy and content in our homes. Do not worry about what is happening in some corner of the world. Come on, won't you give us a smile?

So saying, Bharathiyar sent me away. But, they were talking until nine o'clock.

'How Did You Go?'

As days went by, the police in Puducherry stepped up surveillance and restrictions on *swadeshis* like Bharathiyar. Money orders and letters were not delivered to them. The letters we sent from Puduvai were burnt in Villupuram and we learnt about it only a week later from a few well-meaning workers in the post office.

In such trying times, Bharathiyar was gearing up to bring out the second edition of his *Panchali Sabatham*-Part I (The Vow of Panchali). He had sold or given away all the copies of the first edition without keeping even a single copy for himself. More copies were given away as gifts than were sold. Even the handwritten original draft was missing. Bharathiyar came home one day to find out whether Iyer or my father happened to have a copy. They did not have it either.

Iyer was upset. 'This is ridiculous Bharathi. Can't you keep at least one copy for yourself?'

Bharathiyar said, 'I thought I had a copy in the house. I can compose it again, but it may not turn out exactly like the earlier version. Let it be. I'll compose again'.

My father said, 'Don't any of the children have it? They might have kept one for themselves because the cover was really attractive. Why don't you ask Yadhugiri?'

Bharathiyar called me and asked, 'Yadhugiri, do you have a copy of *Panchali Sabatham*?'

'I have. But I will not give it to anyone. You left my copy of *Aadhi Parvam* in somebody's house. It never came back to me. I will not give this to you,' I said.

'I will give you a new copy of *Aadhi Parvam*. You are a *samaya sanjeevi*. Saved me at the right time. I will give you a much better copy. Please give me your copy of *Panchali Sabatham*,' Bharathiyar pleaded. I brought my copy from the cupboard. Bharathiyar was pleasantly surprised that I had covered the book with paper so that the cover of the book would not get dirty.

'Bharathi wants this badly. Give it to him. When the new edition gets published, he will certainly give you a new copy,' my father said.

I did not have the heart to part with the book. 'I do not want a new copy. I want only this copy. Return this to me as soon as the work is done,' I said. Bharathiyar agreed.

But the book never came back to me. The first page had the

following inscription on it in Bharathiyar's handwriting, 'Given to Miss Yadhugiri Devi with Love – C. Subramania Bharathi'.

Whenever Bharathiyar published a book, even if it was in English, he would give me a copy. Iyer also has given me books such as *Mangaiyarkarasi* and *Chandra Guptan*. But he would never write anything on the books.

It is a wonder to me how the Bharathiyar household managed to survive in those difficult times. I didn't even think about such things then. I used to frequently ask my father why Bharathiyar had not composed any new songs. My father would reply that he was probably busy with some other work.

One day, I could hear Bharathiyar's voice upstairs. I ran to him eagerly like the Jacobin cuckoo would meet the rain. He affectionately made me sit by his side.

Bharathi: Earlier, when I used to sing, Yadhugiri did not show so much interest. Look at her eagerness now.

Sri Sri: Yadhugiri has been asking me why you had not been composing any new songs. I told her that you were busy with other work.

Bharathi: It was not because of work. Rajaram[4] had asked me to go through his father's translation of an Upanishad and correct that draft. It took nearly three months. Only now have I been able to get back to even worshipping Saraswathi.

4 A friend in Puduvai. Refer to opening lines in the song Guru Darisanam – *Bharathi in 66*

Iyer came into the room just as Bharathiyar finished singing the song *Enganam Sendrirundheer* (How Did You Go?) in *Nondi Sindhu* tune. He sang it once more for him.

Iyer: It is beautiful. You have compressed the events of four or five months succinctly in just five lines.

Sri Sri: No one else has the power to condense and convey multiple meanings in just a single line like Bharathi.

Bharathi: The four of us have our own special gifts. You say that I sing well. I say that there is no other writer like you. We say that there is no better translation expert than Iyer. We both say that no one can translate old scriptures into English and compile them like Babu (Sri Aurobindo Ghosh). The four of us are skilled in four different disciplines.

Sri Sri: Our time will come. Let's not be in a hurry and get anxious. These are difficult times.

Iyer: When the gods churned the ocean for *amirtham*, it was poison that emerged first. For those who tread new paths, there will always be difficulties in the beginning. There is no better example of that than us. If one works with determination without losing heart, he or she will certainly find *amirtham*.

Bharathi: We don't even receive appreciative letters. Chellamma wants to go to her native place.

Sri Sri: What he says is right. Today, you have prayed to Saraswathi. Tomorrow, you will hear from *Swadesamitran*.

Don't worry!

The next day Chellamma came to our house. She looked happy.

Chellamma: Good news! There was a letter from *Swadesamitran* asking for an article. Money that had been blocked for the past three months has also arrived. What your father said yesterday has come true.

Me: Bharathiyar told me that you wanted to go to your native place. I was wondering whether you were expecting a baby.

Chellamma: God will not keep creating difficulties all the time Yadhugiri. These two children are enough for me. He will not add to our difficulties.

Me: Don't you want a son?

Chellamma: These girls can do the rituals as well as boys. Look at him. He wears no sacred thread. Does not perform the rituals to either forefathers or Gods. Let's see how a male child, if born to me, would do all funeral rites for me.

Me: But doesn't he wear the sacred thread?

Chellamma: He stopped wearing it when Sakuntala was born. According to him, the sacred thread is meant only for those who do puja and other ritual rites. He returned it to the teacher.

By then, Bharathiyar had also arrived. Chellamma told Bharathiyar about the conversation we had.

Bharathi: We will see later on what a son can do. There is a saying that a daughter is hundred times more precious than a son. There is a proverb in English too, "A son will remain a son only until his wife comes, but a daughter will remain a daughter until death". What have I done for my father? So what can I expect of a son?

We talked about many things and returned home by eight o'clock. Bharathiyar's conversation that day smacked of frustration and bitterness.

India, One of the Best Countries in the World

One day Balu, a friend of ours, came to our house and said, 'Chellamma has been crying inconsolably. She has not had any food since yesterday and she will not listen to us'. My father took me along to Bharathiyar's house. Bharathiyar was getting bored with Puducherry. He was obsessed with the desire to travel to different places. He did not tell Chellamma anything about this. Maybe my father knew about his plans.

Bharathiyar had set out after shaving off his moustache and beard to hide his identity. Chellamma waited at home for one full day in anxiety. When Balu went there, he realised that she had not eaten any food at all.

I asked Chellamma to come to our house. 'I am not afraid of being here alone. I am worried about him. He is too impulsive in all that he does. What if the policemen recognise him and find out his real identity? Look how wilful he is! He didn't even care to share his plans with me, his wife, and I had trusted him all along'.

My father was always hesitant to talk to women from other families. He said, 'Yadhugiri, tell her that there is no need to be afraid. Maybe, he did not tell her about his plans because he thought she might get scared. He is smart. He will not get caught so easily. It must be hard for her to be alone. Ask her to come to our house with the child. We have plenty of space'.

'I am not finding it difficult here. Our neighbours are very good and friendly. I am just terribly worried for him. I will write to my father and brother and will go to my native place. What will I do here without him?' said Chellamma.

My father gave me ten rupees to give to Chellamma and asked me to stay back with her. I spent that day in Bharathiyar's house. Chellamma got up to cook food for me. Bharathiyar's daughter Sakuntala had food at her sister-in-law's house. The other daughter Thangamma was with her aunt in Kasi. I requested Chellamma again to come to our house.

Chellamma: No Yadhugiri. I cannot leave everything here and go with you. Ever since we got married, people have been advising him not to join this swadeshi movement, but he was very stubborn. Because of that, we had to leave our house, our town behind, and settle down here. We are spied upon, the policemen have intercepted our postal letters and have made life difficult for us. Where is the need to go looking for trouble? If he gets caught and is sent to places like the Andaman Islands, what can we do? Who can help us then? Who do we have?

Me: Why are you getting scared Chellamma? He will come back.

Chellamma: He cannot remain quiet. My father used to say, "God Kumaran can melt away travails that seem as huge as mountains". He is our only support now.

Me: Shall I go home Chellamma?

Chellamma: Please don't. Stay here with me. I will come with you to your house in the evening. I'll while away the time chatting with you for a while.

We talked about various things and finished eating. Va.Ve.Su. Iyer's wife Bhagyalakshmi Ammal arrived then. All three of us sat on a mat in the courtyard.

Bhagyalakshmi Ammal: Chellamma, come to our house. You should not be here alone. We will also have something to do looking after you.

Chellamma: I am least worried about myself. My sister-in-law is also with us. Her children are hovering around me all the time. Sakuntala is like her child. My thoughts are all about him and the daring risk he has taken.

Bhagyalakshmi Ammal: You are upset even by this. Can you imagine how I would have felt when he (Iyer) went overseas?

Chellamma: If he could keep his emotions under control like Iyer, I would not be worried. What if something stirs him and he breaks into a song?

Bhagyalakshmi Ammal: What you say is also right. He would not do such things. He probably would go around, see the places where he had lived and get back.

Chellamma: What is the use of me getting anxious? Everything will happen according to fate. For instance, Dr Nanjunda Rao is a dear friend of his. But when it came to the swadeshi movement, he ignored his advice too. Who knows what difficulties are still in store for us?

Me: Let us speak only of good things Chellamma. God will not forsake us. If we do good, we will only reap good.

Chellamma shifted to our home in the evening. Around ten to fifteen days passed by.

One day I went upstairs and found a stranger talking to my father. I was sitting at the table and working on my lessons. The stranger turned to me and asked, 'Where is my offering?' I was startled. 'Even you are not able to recognise me?' he asked.

Me: Is that you, Bharathiyar? Poor Chellamma was traumatised and went through hell. How can you do this to her?

Bharathi: What did I do? Even you, who usually come running to me, could not recognise me! How could the C.I.Ds have recognised me?

I paid his usual offering and asked, 'Where were you? Tell me, tell me about everything you saw'.

Bharathi: I will tell you leisurely. I hear that it was you who stood by Chellamma and gave her courage these last few days?

Me: Courage? She does not want to be courageous. She didn't even eat. I asked her to come home and she refused.

Bharathi: What can I do, if she refused to come to your house? I went away counting on your strength and support. If I had told her my plans earlier, she would have prevented me from going.

Me: Have you written any new songs?

Bharathi: Even while I was going by train, I had composed one. I controlled myself often because I was afraid I would sing it aloud. I will sing that song tomorrow. I have a cold and a sore throat now.

As promised, Bharathiyar sang his new song the next day, the nationalist song that begins with *Paarukkulle Nalla Naadu* (India, One of the Best Countries in the World). When he was travelling by train, a beggar woman was singing a Hindustani song. He had composed the poem in the same tune.

During Bharathiyar's absence, Chellamma had not eaten regularly and had gone thin. Chellamma's father took Chellamma and Sakuntala away with him to Kadayam, saying that his daughter was afflicted by an aversion to food and would not survive if she continued to stay there.

Bharathiyar did not have a problem with that. He would eat whenever someone invited him to eat without fuss. Chellamma came back after two months. On arrival, she said, 'He has no worries at all. He has friends all over the place. I came back because I thought he was suffering, but he turns around and asks me why I had returned so soon and that he has no objection to me being happy in my father's place. I do not know what kind of a man he is'.

Chellamma brought back her first daughter Thangamma with her. As a child, Thangamma grew up in a tradition-bound household. So Bharathiyar and Thangamma would enter into heated arguments and he would always win. Thangamma would eventually cool down and give up because he was, after all, her father.

The Sermon

It was a time of the waxing moon. As usual, we went to the beach in the evening. Padmavathi, Sankara Chettiar's (another Puduvai philanthropist, like Ponnu Murugesam Pillai; a close friend of Bharathiyar and Aurobindo) daughter, was an acquaintance of mine. My mother, sister, Thangamma, Chellamma, Padmavathi, and Meena used to go to the beach every day and return home by seven or eight.

That day, my father had chest pain and my mother did not accompany us to the beach. We were sitting on the beach and chatting when Iyer and Bharathiyar came from Aurobindo's house. Iyer didn't want to disturb the women and so stood at a distance talking to somebody else. Bharathiyar alone approached us.

Bharathi: I hope I am not intruding...

Chellamma: Not at all. They are all our children. Padmavathi, too, is only a child.

Bharathiyar came next to us and sat by our side.

Bharathi: How come Yadhugiri is not to be seen these days like before? Looks like she has become part of the women's group.

Chellamma: Didn't you know? They are going to get her married in the month of Chithirai. They are searching for a suitable boy. When she goes to the mother-in-law's house, can she mingle as before with men? So she is learning to be submissive now itself.

Bharathi: When is the marriage?

Me: I do not know. My grandmother has taken a decision. Amma has asked me not to talk to men other than Iyer and Bharathiyar.

Bharathi: What is wrong if you speak to other men?

Me: I do not know. That is what my mother told me.

Chellamma: They have brought her up like a male child. It will be difficult for her at first when she goes to her mother-in-law's house. It will be easier if she gets used to restraints now itself.

Bharathi: But she is a small child. Srinivasaachariyar is an old-fashioned man. Yadhugiri is but a child who has no experience of the world, yet he is planning a *bommai kalyanam* for her.

Chellamma: The sastras say Brahmins should get married by the time they are nine. Nowadays, they take their time because it is not convenient.

Bharathi: There are a number of such traditions and customs. Why don't you arrange Thangam's marriage too, a meaningless mockery of marriage.

Chellamma: It was my sister who brought up Thangam and she will do the needful.

Bharathi: Yadhugiri, hereafter, you'll be living in a different world.

Chellamma: Why, won't she visit us at all after marriage?

Bharathi: Chellamma, can I move with Yadhugiri the same way after her marriage? I will need her husband's permission.

Chellamma: Why think about it now? We will deal with that after she gets married.

Bharathi: Yadhugiri, we have known you ever since you were a child and have brought you up ourselves but if I come to your mother-in-law's house, the people there may raise objections and forbid you to talk to a 'stranger'. You do not know the ways of the world Yadhugiri. So far you have seen only one world. The world you are going to is a totally different one. They follow century-old customs and practices there. In our houses, we have so much freedom. We have left our homes and native towns and are living here just to preserve that freedom. It will take at least thirty years for other families to reach the stage we have reached. Until then, you may have to follow the old ways.

Chellamma: You sound as if you are talking to convicts going to jail. She will get frightened.

Bharathi: She is not aware of the difficulties, inequalities, and other foolish practices in the world out there. In our community, upon getting married, couples start their own homes. That practice has not started yet in the Mandaiyathar clan.

Chellamma: Aha! It is five years since I came away from a joint family.

Bharathi: Those were the old days. In Tirunelveli yesterday, I saw that all the families were nuclear families. Not even a single joint family. Let that be. Do you want this marriage Yadhugiri?

Me: I do not know anything. This is my parents' decision. When they themselves still follow my grandmother's wishes, my likes and dislikes do not matter.

Bharathi: Have they found a boy? Have you seen him?

Me: I haven't seen anyone. Letters have arrived from four or five families. Mother wants one thing, and grandmother wants another. My father wants them to arrive at a joint decision. That is all that I know.

Bharathi: Our marriage also happened the same way. But nowadays, it is fashionable for boys to marry educated girls. Has that practice not spread in your community yet?

Me: We have not given up the old customs yet. Girls do study but only at home. They do not go to school. Two or three daughters of big officials go to schools to study.

Bharathi: Then, it looks like the marriage will go ahead. Do not forget me Yadhugiri! When the husband is by your side, you tend to forget everything else. Do remember this poor father now and then.

Me: Can I ever forget you? Even if you are poor, your songs are the greatest. Iyer asked me yesterday, 'Why not call Bharathi the King of Poetry?' Wealth is impermanent, it will come and go, but songs are forever; they will live on in people's hearts.

Bharathi: If I have a few *shishyas* like you, I don't have to get my songs printed at all. You have literally memorised all my songs. Chellamma, I will sing a patriotic song during Yadhugiri's marriage. That will be my gift. If we can afford it then, we will make the event unforgettable.

Chellamma: Your heart is bigger than the ocean. If we are fortunate, we will give her a grand gift.

Me: What can be a bigger gift than your songs? My father is not keeping well at all. You and Iyer will have to run around and make all the arrangements for the marriage.

Bharathi: We will take care of all the work outside. But they will not let us into the kitchen.

Me: My grandmother will take care of that. She will want lots of people at the marriage. She cannot bear it if there are only a few at the function. She has the ability to administer a kingdom.

Bharathiyar then gave me a big sermon.

'Yadhugiri, I will give you a few pieces of advice. Do not forget them. Chastity is very important for women. It is your primary duty to protect it more carefully than your own life. That does not mean that you have to live like a caged parrot. All men except your husband are brothers. You do not have to be shy or timid or avoid men or be afraid of them. You should talk freely with everyone. You may be shy with your husband in the beginning, but you do not need to be as days go by. It has been dinned into our women that fear, shyness, and modesty are essential feminine virtues. Women and men have internalised that and have thoroughly immersed themselves in a life of subordination. Your children will grow to be bold only if you are bold. Cowardice has destroyed India's greatness, helped along by the passage of time.

You should remain bold even after you go to your in-laws' house. Don't be scared of anything. Don't eavesdrop. Don't read the letters of others. Be direct in expressing your views. It is better to be open and talk frankly than hide your feelings and feel wretched. Try your best to obey them. If you cannot, let them know clearly. Don't hide anything. A lot of good can come out of such frankness. They have not bought you. You are going to help develop and perfect their household. You have every right in that house. Don't interfere in money matters. Leave that to the elders. Don't hesitate to work. But don't take on something which is beyond your ability. Put your heart into everything you do. Do not give up your studies. Your parents have taught you important and universal truths with great difficulty. If you can, improve upon it. If you can't, don't forget what you already know.

I will not preach sacrifice like Iyer. You should enjoy all the pleasures this world has to offer and, in turn, be useful to the world. I am totally against the notion of seeking fulfilment in sacrifice.

You should shine like a bright light on both houses. To start with, it will be hard to integrate two families' lives together. Eventually, you will get used to it. Never let yourself be treated like a slave. You have rights. You have brains. You have freedom. Walk with your head held high. Enjoy the pleasures of nature. Look everybody straight in the eye. The husband is the only person who deserves a sideways glance from you. Look at your father, brothers, children, and others straight in the eye. Sit straight. Speak boldly. You do not lose your chastity by being bold. There is no need to be fake.'

Bharathiyar gave a lot of such advice. I practised them as holy dictates. During certain difficult times, his words have emboldened and strengthened me. During some sleepless nights, I have wondered whether these words would die with me.

I have written these down for my satisfaction and also because I think they would be useful to other women. Even if he is no more, I want his words to keep resounding in this world.

The Sacred Feet of Kannan

Bharathiyar's life was inseparable from that of our family for ten to twelve years. When talking about him, I cannot help including stories from our lives as well. Like the twine that also gains fragrance because it is used to string flowers together.

My wedding took place in the Kalavai bungalow on 24 April 1913. At around two o'clock the night before, my father's chest pain became intense. Different types of medical treatments were tried out all through the night. In the morning, Bharathiyar brought Kalavai Sankara Chettiar and a French doctor called Ambu home. The doctor prescribed some medicines that Bharathiyar himself bought from the medical shop. My father became a little better by the auspicious time fixed for the marriage.

The wedding ceremony duly took place. Bharathiyar, Iyer, Periya Swamigal Mahavidhwan Karaikal Swami, my periappa and chithappa had all gathered there. After the *mangalya dharanam*, my husband and I sought the blessings of Mahavidhwan Karaikal Swami first, and that of Bharathiyar and Iyer next. We then went on to seek the blessings of other relatives.

The evil of dowry was not as widespread in our community back then as it is now. Whatever the bride's family gave as a token of respect was happily accepted. The marriage ceremony went on for five days peacefully without any quarrels breaking out or much clamour. Bharathiyar and Chellamma worked tirelessly, making sure that all the arrangements were in place.

On the first day, there was the *muhurtham*, along with rituals on the swing, and some other rituals like the rolling of coconuts, *aupasanam*, and so on. On the second day, the highlight was Bharathiyar's invaluable and sweet rendering of a patriotic song. On the third day, a person called Thiruvengadathan mimicked the sound of the flute with his voice. On the fourth day, we were treated to a music performance by my aunt, who was the eldest of the women in the family and an accomplished artist.

After my marriage, a series of happy events took place—the marriages of my elder brother, my younger sister, and my aunt's daughter took place in Chennai. Chellamma's sister Swarnam's marriage also took place around that time. Chellamma, who was away for two months in connection with that, returned with Thangamma. Our families were entirely involved in these wedding functions for about three months.

After a few days, my grandfather, grandmother, and older uncle came along with my younger sister to Puducherry. My grandfather is a great scholar blessed with an exceptional gift of storytelling. When he narrates Vaishnavite texts, the listeners forget and lose themselves in the narration. He makes it accessible to even young children.

Bharathiyar and my grandfather would often enter into heated discussions, although he appreciated Bharathiyar's poetic skills and intellectual prowess. My grandfather was in the business of gems. Bharathiyar would get excited when my grandfather explained in detail the qualities of precious stones like diamonds, greenstones, rubies, pearls, etc.

One day, my grandfather talked about the subtle meanings of some of the songs in Nammaazhwar's *Thiruvaimozhi* in *Naalayira Divya Prabandham*. The poetic conventions employed in these songs became imprinted in Bharathiyar's mind. He said that they should be sung, and then he set them to music. Particularly, he would sing with tremendous feeling *Ivaiyum, Avaiyum, Uvaiyum*, the ninetieth song in *Thiruvaimozhi* that meant 'God works through us by entering our physical selves'.

Although my grandfather was not particularly interested in music, listening to Bharathiyar singing with passionate involvement, he would say, 'Aazhwar too must have sung like this. All sins have vanished in this act of singing from memory. Not everybody can sing like Bharathiyar'.

If Bharathiyar talked about ten songs from *Thiruvaimozhi* on the first day, he would set them to music and sing them all the next day. These lessons were a daily routine for me. But I would slip away after learning the tune of the song and before the discussion on Vedanta began because I would not understand it and I had no interest in it either.

For about two months, Iyer, Bharathiyar, Ayya and Chinnaiyya (S.N. Thirumalaachariyar) got to enjoy the greatness of *Thiruvaimozhi* day after day.

After a few days, the ceremony relating to my attaining puberty was conducted. That evening, people were invited and given a gift of turmeric, *kumkumam*, and betel leaves. They performed the *sobanam.* My grandmother regretted that my aunt who could recite the *Thiruvaimozhi* and perform the *kummi* dance was not there. She invited those who knew how to sing to come forward and perform the *kummi.*

An older married woman sang five songs from *Thiruvaimozhi* starting with *Kannan Kazhalinai* and danced the *kummi.* Bharathiyar was watching this from upstairs. After the *kummi* dance got over, he argued over many issues with my grandfather.

Bharathiyar came home the next evening too. He was singing one of his recently composed songs to my grandfather. I was about to go upstairs to join them when my grandmother stopped me saying that henceforth I should not mingle with men.

As I did not go upstairs even after Bharathiyar sang the song twice, he came downstairs. I was sitting with others. 'Why Yadhugiri, are you not feeling well child?' asked Bharathiyar. I gave a sheepish smile and said, 'Nothing like that'.

'Why didn't you come upstairs, child?'
'My grandmother asked me not to.'

'Grandma, I am not a stranger. Yadhugiri is our child too. She does not have to hide herself from us. Do children feel shy with their fathers? Here, Yadhugiri'. So saying, he gave me a note and went back upstairs. I found the song titled *Maname* (O Heart), beginning with the line 'Think of the sacred feet of Kannan, O heart' in the note.

Sakthi Explained

Murugesam Pillai's family diligently followed old customs and practices. On new moon and full moon days, Fridays and on the days of an eclipse, they would give offerings to the gods and alms to the poor and mendicants, mainly rice, coconut, jaggery, and pulses.

Bharathiyar did not like this practice, saying people followed it blindly. He used to say there were no gods or demons and that beggars and mendicants were usually idlers and cheats. 'Give alms to the lame, the blind, and the old. Do not give it to these idlers and fake priests,' he would say.

The man who first won Bharathiyar over among them was the *kulla* swamiyar. He slowly started speaking to Bharathiyar while he was visiting Murugesam Pillai's house. Whether some good came out of this acquaintance or not, Bharathiyar from then on began to move with the group of priests. Bharathiyar, who was always looking for new ways of doing things, found a guide in this *kulla* swami.

In our region, it was common practice to keep two earthen lamps lit on every street in the evening, from Deepavali to the day on which the Karthigai light would be extinguished in Thiruvannamalai. In Murugesam Pillai's house, two lamps would be lit on the first day and then two more each day. They would only stop when the Thiruvannamalai light was put out.

One Friday evening, Meena, Padmavathi, my sisters and I went to Bharathiyar's house. His house was four houses away from Murugesam Pillai's house. Chellamma was losing her temper with *vaanichi*, the woman who sold oil.

Vaanichi: Today, we didn't get a slot to press the oil amma. I will definitely bring it tomorrow.

Chellamma: Today is Friday. There is no oil to light the street lamp. I have been asking you for the last four days. I didn't ask my sister-in-law also for oil thinking that you will bring it. Nobody will give oil now as it is already time to light the lamp.

Vaanichi: What can I do amma? I waited at the oil mill for a long time and got fed up. What can I do?

Bharathiyar, who was in the front room, was listening to this conversation.

Bharathi: It is not the end of the world Chellamma. Why don't you light two candles instead? What is the use of getting angry with her if the oil mill was crowded today?

Chellamma: Lighting candles when everybody else lights oil lamps? Everything is upside down here. Candles are made of fish oil, using that will be...pollution! Will Goddess Lakshmi come to such a house? Girl, go to the shop and buy some oil.

Bharathi: Chellamma, why do we need a lamp now? We have an electric lamp post right in front of our house. Lakshmi will come to our house even for that light. Do not send the poor servant girl out now. It may rain today.

Chellamma: It is my headache. Why do you interfere? The servant girl will not get drenched if she goes to the shop nearby.

Bharathi: You keep this hurricane lamp in the street. That is enough.

Chellamma: Kerosene is also pollution. We need oil meant for this purpose only. There will be no soot, it will burn well, and it is good for the eyes. If you want to pick a quarrel with me over this, I will not light a lamp at all. Hey girl, you go home. If you get wet in the rain, Iyer seems to feel the cold. Go to your house.

Bharathi: Look, children. Chellamma gets angry if I tell it as it is. What can we do if she considers candles and kerosene impure?

Me: Women believe that old customs and practices are good for us. Won't Chellamma get angry if you suddenly try to introduce new ones like lighting a candle or a hand lamp?

Chellamma: Tell me Yadhugiri. When we live in a society, shouldn't we also follow its customs? In my sister-in-law's house, they have lit twenty lamps. Shouldn't we at least light two?

Bharathi: And a quarrel materialises to while away the time. Tell me, why do we light lamps?

Chellammal: During these months, Goddesses Sakthi, Ambal, Lakshmi, Gangai, and others come in a procession in the evenings. They will choose to reside in houses that are clean, tidy, and neat.

Meena: Lamps should be lit in all the houses until the flame in Thiruvannamalai is put out. My grandmother used to say that even if we cannot afford to light the lamps all through the year, if we do it as per tradition from Deepavali to Karthigai, Parvathi, Lakshmi, and Gangai will reside in our houses.

Bharathi: No, the reason is totally different. In the name of tradition and customs, we forget the real reason. Earlier, we had no permanent street lights. And it gets very dark during the rainy season. If lamps are lit in all the houses in a row, it will light up three-fourths of the village, dispelling the darkness. Our elders did this with this purpose in mind. Now that we have electric lights in every street, tell me where is the need for these lamps? Is it right to say that since our grandfathers grew up in the dark, we will also grow up similarly? Lakshmi does not care for oil lamps, dirt, purity, false beliefs without a rational basis, pretences, etc. Your love, genuine devotion, and singing with strong faith and determination are all that Lakshmi values. She will not be duped by extravagance. Today, all the children have gathered here. Let them sing whatever song they like. I will also join in. Chellamma, light two candles. Lakshmi will definitely come to this house. Keep a picture of Lakshmi on the chair. You join too Chellamma. Let us all sing.

Chellamma did so half-heartedly. We sang the songs with which we were familiar. Bharathiyar sang the song *Vande Matharam*. Then he said, 'I will now sing a new song line by line. You can also join me and sing along. There cannot be better worship than that'. We sang as he requested. It was the song titled *Sakthi Vilakkam* (Sakthi Explained) that begins with the sentence '*Adi Paramporulin Vookkam*'.

When nine voices sang in unison, the whole street began to gather there. Bharathiyar's sister-in-law, too, came to his house thinking that we were all dancing the *kummi*. Chellamma spread a mat and we all sat there. For about two hours, we sang Bharathiyar's songs and worshipped together.

Bharathi: Today Lakshmi has really visited our house. Chellamma, why don't you distribute turmeric and *kumkumam*?

Chellamma: You said it will rain today. But your *bhajanai* has scared the rain away.

Bharathi: It will definitely rain tonight Chellamma. Send the children home soon.

We went home after receiving turmeric and *kumkumam*. It rained heavily the moment we reached home.

Just as Bharathiyar said, Lakshmi did visit his house that day. However, she did not stay there permanently. She came in and went out as she pleased.

May Bharatha Society Thrive

Just before the Pongal festival, tonnes of different kinds of food grain could be found stored in Ponnu Murugesam Pillai's house. Iyer and Bharathiyar would buy what was needed for that year from that stock. Because he had a high esteem for Iyer and Bharathiyar as *swadeshis*, Pillai would give them a special discount.

One day, I was on my way to Bharathiyar's house, when Iyer and Bharathiyar saw me on the way and took me along to Murugesam Pillai's house. Pillai spread a mat for us to sit on and placed a plate of betel leaves before us. After talking about various things, Iyer inquired about the prices of pulses. 'I do not know what the going rates are in town, but whatever it is, you know that there is always a special discount for you. I will send word when the Pongal puja and the distribution to the *muraikarargal* are done'.

From there, we came to Bharathiyar's house. I asked him the

meaning of *muraikarargal.* Bharathiyar explained the village practice patiently.

Bharathi: Ours is an agricultural country. The main aim is to feed all the people and prevent starvation. If people have money, they would spend it all away. But, with grains, people can store whatever they need for their families for the year except for salt. When a Zamindar harvests his fields, for example, a certain quantity of paddy will be set aside for labourers, washermen, sanitary workers, Brahmins who perform pujas, temple priests, village schoolteachers, barbers and others as the wages for the whole year. This kind of distribution of grains can be managed easily and it is also good for those who receive their wages this way. Their basic food needs for the whole year are taken care of. There is no household that does not have its priests, dhobis, cleaners, teachers, or barbers. When common people are given five measures of rice per house, they will have sufficient quantity. According to our sastras, whatever difficulties we might have will vanish if we donate sesame seeds and urad dal. Sesame seeds are nutritionally very vital for the poor.

When the new year dawns, we keep what we require for our consumption and give away the rest to the above-mentioned workers in return for their labour. Such recipients are called *muraikarargal.* As Murugesam Pillai's family has lived here for generations, he continues this practice.

Me: Won't money be a better compensation instead?

Bharathi: Maybe. We should keep ten or fifteen rupees in hand during Pongal. Labourers and conch-blowers will ask for new clothes. We have to give money to dhobis, barbers, cleaners and others. If we don't have cash, it will be hard to send them away empty-handed. But then, money is not of much use. Even if they receive ten rupees in total, they will not buy paddy or things needed for the year with it. They will spend it carelessly. There will be constant complaints at home about the family's needs. If you pay them in kind, they cannot sell it immediately and so they'll have to stock it at home. So this is a better way.

This is a very good arrangement made by our elders for people like us who do not have landed property. People will help the farmers when they realise that there will be grains in their houses only if they do farming.

Me: In our place, people keep four kinds of cooked rice by the ponds the day after Pongal. What is that for?

Bharathi: See that Iyer with the beard? Ask him. I do not really know. He would have read the sastras and may know the answer. I totally dislike customs, sastras, and mythologies. You asked me about *muraikarargal* and I told you what I knew. Iyer will answer your second question.

Iyer: I will tell you Yadhugiri. Birds and fish help a great deal in saving our crops from pests. When we harvest the produce, we prepare food in the temple, make our offerings to Amman first and assume that Amman takes the food directly to the ponds for the birds and fish to make them happy.

In the south, pregnant women who have prayed for a female child would be invited during the Kanu festival and made to feed all the creatures, especially cows, birds, fish, frogs, etc. with their own hands. They would then be given some things to help them bring up a girl child, like grains, money, clothes, or whatever they can afford and then would be taken to the house of the in-laws.

Pongal is a festival during which we fill our stomachs to our heart's content. Nowadays, it is totally different though. What does the man who earns only ten rupees a month know about the joys of this festival? For him, all days are alike. If he is frugal, he can save a little and buy extra groceries. Otherwise, his salary will be just enough for his daily needs.

Bharathi: Tell me Iyer, if he buys groceries in bigger quantities, where will he keep them? Won't he need a proper storage place? Can he store them in a hut for which he pays a rupee as rent? How can he protect them from rats and bandicoots?

Iyer: You are right too. But, a man cannot fill his stomach without working hard. It is especially difficult for a generous person like you. A man who lives and manages in a small hut will know the difficulties of others. Even if he becomes wealthy later, he will know the value of saving. When you pass on what you get freely, you don't always know the worth of things.

Bharathi: Chellamma says that we could process pulses ourselves from grains. But I do not like it. By the time you go through the whole process, dry, break and make it edible, the whole house becomes dusty and dirty. If we tell the Chettiar lady, she will bring good pulses and we do not have to sweat. We don't even have to worry about winnowing.

Iyer: Doesn't the Chettiar lady make a profit? What you get from her for ten rupees for a year can be prepared at home for just five or six rupees. We can save four rupees. Nobody will sell without charging us extra for their labour.

Bharathi: Isn't it only proper that those who work hard make a profit?

Iyer: The arrangement is good if we have a lot of money. But, I firmly believe that if we do not, there's no harm in doing this work ourselves. It is good to buy tamarind, lentils, rice, chillies, etc. in large quantities and buy other small items whenever convenient.

Bharathi: People at home have no energy to even cook the already pounded rice.

Iyer: That is the problem with losing touch with our customs. After all, if we cannot do it at all, we can always get it done with the help of servant women.

Bharathi: That is also a big responsibility. If the servants do not measure up to their standards, there will be constant complaints. Your suggestion will work for those who have their houses and land in the same place. They lead a very convenient life. But it is difficult for people like us.

Iyer: It is important to honour good practices. Even if we cannot practise that way of life, we should encourage it and not find fault with it.

Bharathi: I don't think that will ever happen in my life. I asked Chellamma to throw away the iron and stone pots and pans and use glass and porcelain containers like the white people. She tells tall stories of how they have poison in them and that they would break easily.

Iyer: There is truth in what she says. I used to be crazier about them than you. When I was living alone in Rangoon, once I lit the spirit stove, and instead of a brass pot, kept a glass tumbler full of water and went to the other room for tea leaves. When I returned, the tumbler had broken to pieces and the stove too got spoilt. I had to buy a new stove. They have found that porcelain has TB-inducing poisonous ingredients. Our old ways are the best. There is no need to go by glamour.

Bharathi: You are defending Chellamma as if you are her lawyer, singing the praise of old customs and practices. A new year has dawned. Don't you want to hear a new song?

Then he sang the new song, *Bharatha Samudhayam Vaazhgave* (May Bharatha Society Thrive). After talking for a while, we got ready to leave for our homes. All the way back, Iyer was explaining the song to me and praising the powerful lines, 'Even if a single person goes hungry, we will destroy the whole world'.

Women's Education

There arose an interest in women's education in India around 1914. It was accompanied by the call for women's liberation. Some people refused to entertain the very idea.

There was a general feeling that women should not be learning English. But a few had, even then, come forward in support of women's education. Some people who were in high positions ignored Vedic restrictions and sent their daughters to school to learn English. Some others warned that this could lead to the end of the world. Young widows also enrolled themselves in large numbers in schools. Some complained that the price of *appalams* had gone up from four *anna*s to eight *anna*s for a hundred pieces in Vaikunta Vathiyar Street as a result!

Some folks who were afraid of society's backlash but eager to educate their women got British women to visit their homes and teach basic English to them. Our community, too, underwent many changes. Those who vociferously condemned this earlier were now taking the lead in giving priority to women's education. From 1914-15 onwards, our relatives also started sending women to English schools.

After dinner, my father used to tell me and my brother the story of *The Count of Monte Cristo* by Alexander Dumas, the plays by Shakespeare and Moliere, about *Gil Blas,* and others. My father had even translated some sections of *Gil Blas*. We used to eagerly look forward to these sessions.

Leaving aside how others reacted to the issue of women's education, it invigorated Bharathiyar. He had always been seeking new words, and new ways to approach life. This movement made him feel as if he had two additional shoulders to take on more work. He used to say that more than education, women could benefit more from widow remarriage and the abolition of child marriage. 'There is no need for women to be educated as highly as men,' he would say. According to him, it was more important for them to be courageous, civilised, and clean. Bharathiyar has portrayed the greatness and dignity of women to the greatest extent possible in his poems.

I was eager to go to school with the other girls in my age group. I fought with my mother to let me go to school. She said categorically, 'No. You can learn from your father at home'. I cried a lot that day and created a ruckus at home.

That evening, Bharathiyar and Chellamma came home by four. We went to the beach as usual. I sat there with a long, grim face.

Bharathi: What happened Yadhugiri? Why are you upset? You are not your usual self. Did your mother get angry with you about something?

I did not say anything but started crying inconsolably. Chellamma laid my head on her lap and tried to console me. After a while, I said, 'Chellamma, all my friends have joined a school to learn English. I told my mother that I too wanted to join but she said, no'.

Chellamma: Is that the reason you are upset? Crazy girl. Those girls may not have come of age even if they are the same age as you. It is not good to send girls who have attained puberty to school. Moreover, your in-laws may not approve of it. Don't you have to think about all this Yadhugiri?

Bharathi: Are you inferior to them in any way just because your peers are going to school and you are not? The lessons taught there about England's countryside, rivers, lakes, etc. are irrelevant to our lives here. Learn Tamil well, that is enough. If you go to school, you may be drawn to certain bad habits. Women stand to gain nothing from that.

Me: What are you saying? Do you think all the other girls go to school in order to gain nothing? Do you think everyone except us is a fool?

Chellamma: Are you planning to work after your studies? My father used to say that it was enough if we learned to check accounts and read and write letters. But now people read epics, poetry, and novels. The languages of our country are important to us. Men need to learn English in order to read letters. They may even read insignificant novels. But, you can do the same thing by learning Sanskrit, Telugu, Kannada, and Hindi.

Me: Nowadays, everything important is published in English. My grandmother used to say that Telugu is as mellifluous as honey, Kannada is as fragrant as kasthuri, and Tamil is unyielding and hard. I have often fought with her saying some of the best poems can be found in Tamil.

Bharathi: The fault is not with your grandmother Yadhugiri. Like you said, Tamils are now going crazy over English. People have added newly translated words from other languages to Kannada and Telugu. Tamil, which was once superior, is at the bottom rung now. So they make fun of Tamil as a difficult language.

Me: Why has it reached such a low level?

Bharathi: The reasons are many. Tamils lack the will and are indifferent to their own poetry once they learn English. It is difficult to read and understand poetry. Also, there are very few people to financially support Tamil and encourage its development. Bengalis pour a lot of money into developing their language. Though a few Tamils are wealthy, they do not feel like supporting the cause of Tamil. They spend their lives guarding their wealth. What can we do about that? Parents spend all that they have to educate their children, counting on their future earnings. But what the children earn is not enough even for themselves. How can they compensate their parents? Under these circumstances, they do not have the time to think about whether Tamil is still alive or dead. In this land of dearth, if people stand up for a cause, they are viewed as enemies of both the state and their community.

Chellamma: It is *kaliyugam*. Everything has turned upside down. There is chaos everywhere!

Bharathi: No this is the Vedic age Chellamma! Demands abound in the Vedas—Destroy the demons; save us from diseases; save our children from diseases; fulfil our desires; let the country flourish; Varuna! Indira! Save our crops from the destruction of demons. Oh…Vayu, you are the real god. The Vedas are nothing but a string of such pleas. It is the same case with the *Quran* of the Muslims. The *Quran* also says, 'Lead our children in the right path. Make them brave! Save us from scarcity of food and clothing! Help us live as equals to others! Bless us with good water, good air!' It is the same with the *Bible*. Only the languages in which they are written are different.

Chellamma: Are *Periya Puranam* and Shankarachariyar's stories all false?

Bharathi: Who said that they are lies? That was the Upanishadic age. People got fed up with nature, which was predictable and remained the same throughout the year, embraced abstinence, and proclaimed the physical world to be false and god, the only truth. And you had the conflict between the Shaivites and the Vaishnavites too. Everyone started preaching the importance of sacrifice. It is a law of nature that the world goes through different eras. With the influence of western culture, our material desires have increased. Western fads have created many kinds of desires even in the minds of small children. After immersing themselves in these fads for a while, people will tire of it. It is natural to crave a new job, a new way of life, or a new fad. After some time, you realise that it is just a meaningless luxury. Until then, such things will keep happening.

Chellamma: Was it like this during the Mughal period?

Bharathi: Akbar treated the Hindus fairly. So did Babar. During his last days, Akbar had warned, 'My descendants may ill-treat Hindus to establish Islam on a firm footing. But, they will not be able to achieve even the little I have accomplished and will turn out to be destroyers of their own faith'. Just like he said, their end followed soon. But the Christians, on the other hand, respected people and talked them into accepting their ways. During the terrible famine in the Thaadhu year, they prepared gruel in large containers, gave a handful to the sick and converted them to Christianity. The pastors in the mission promised lots of money and jobs for those willing to convert, but cheated them and left them in the lurch.

Chellamma: Yet, you say that all religions are equal?

Bharathi: That's right. So? Did I say that we should give up wearing *kumkumam* and turmeric and live like them? Whatever is good in this world belongs to everyone equally. But, we should practise what is suitable in our context. Yadhugiri wants to learn English and you prevent it.

Me: But, are you happy with my decision?

Bharathi: Even I do not like it. If all of us work together for the growth of Tamil, won't it spread globally and get appreciated by everyone? How nice it will be if, rather than feel bad about someone calling it a difficult language, we can all do our part to help in the growth of Tamil with enthusiasm and fervour. That is better than learning English just to lord it over others. It'll benefit us greatly if we introduce and explain new forms of poetry, select and publish famous sayings, translate and publish good literary works from world languages, and translate texts of natural science, environmental and forest science, astronomy, etc. into Tamil.

Me: Ayya told us about a story that had appeared in *Modern Review* with the title, *Kshudhita Pashan*. How do we translate that into Tamil? If we know English, we can read it on our own.

Bharathi: *Kshudhita Pashan* can be 'Hungry Stones/Rocks'.[5] It is a story by Rabindranath Tagore. It is good to translate such emotionally instructive and valuable stories.

Chellamma: The beginning and the ending of the story you narrated the other day, *Maana Bangam,* or *Giri Bala,*[6] do not seem quite right. The story reads like a puzzle. It ends thus, 'Shaking his hands and legs furiously, Gopinathan swears he would kill her. The curtain falls'. We could not understand it completely.

---

5 Bharathiyar had translated this story into Tamil and published it with the title *Asaa Bangam*.

6 Bharathiyar had translated this story too into Tamil.

Bharathi: Chellamma, we are used to stories beginning with, 'Once there lived a king in a town,' and ending with 'he lived happily ever after'. But in this new kind of narrative, like in a cyclone, you only get a fleeting glimpse before it is gone. The meaning will become apparent once we think about it. This is a way to get the readers to read more carefully. You will get used to this once you read a few more stories like this.

Me: For that, we have to learn English or Bengali first. Until then, we have to content ourselves with hearing them from you.

Chellamma: It is so satisfying when he narrates these stories. Some of these stories seem to narrate the very things that happen every day in our houses.

Bharathi: Events from real life are more beautiful than imaginary ones. I have written down what you told the children about the incident at the waterfalls. It was so amusing. I am going to send it to *Swadesamitran*. How the children giggled and laughed at the way you described chithappa. Even our ordinary lives are so full of surprises. If we record them every day, there can be no better stories. It is enough if we keep writing one story like this at a time to enrich Tamil. Srinivasaachariyar wanted to write to Tagore seeking his permission to translate his stories into Tamil. It will be good to get them printed in Tamil.

Bharathiyar sent the story narrated by Chellamma to *Swadesamitran*. It was published in the December 1917 annual special issue with the title *Aruvi, Alladhu Valli Vaana Theerthamaadiya Kadhai*.

On the Altar of Our Sacrifice

The year of happiness, the Ananda year, remained so only in name. It turned out to be a troublesome year, bringing with it a World War and related hardships. There were also big changes in my life. Until I was twelve, I enjoyed my freedom and was the queen in my own house. People pampered me and made sure that I grew up loved without getting hurt.

My new life began in Madras. After a short while, I went with my mother to Puducherry to see my father, spent a week there and returned to Madras.

When I was fourteen, after schools were closed, my husband and I went to Puducherry. He left for Mysore after a week and I stayed back at my mother's house.

The war that began that year continued to rage well into the Ratchasa year. The French scholar Paul Richard had come to Puducherry from Paris. He used to research the Vedas along with Aurobindo Ghosh. He became a close friend of Bharathiyar, Iyer, and my father.

Probably because France was less populated or because of some other reason, the government had passed an order that people with seven children had to join the army. It was Bharathiyar who told us this.

Richard and his family had to leave for Paris because of the new government order. A tea party was arranged to bid them farewell and we all went to the party. Madame Richard, Richard, their two girls and many friends were seated at a round table. There were chairs all around and porcelain plates and bowls were on the table. I had never been to a tea party before. That was my very first experience. We all had tea and snacks except my mother and Bhagyalakshmi Ammal. They chewed betel leaves and areca nuts. After the party, we went to the beach.

Bharathi: Yadhugiri, did you notice a strange thing? Richard and Madame Richard have no children at all. Still, the poor man has to go to war because he is the father of seven. Can you guess why?

Chellamma: What you say does not make sense at all. Their brothers probably have children. Who knows what kind of a law or government order this is.

Bharathi: No Chellamma. There is an interesting angle to it. Richard has three children from his first wife. Madame Richard has four children from her first husband. Because these two are now married, together they have seven children.

Chellamma: Siva, Siva! What a lifestyle! A second marriage when she has four children...Shameful!

Bharathi: It is their culture. Remember I told you that Rabindranath Tagore has written a story called *Maana Bangam*, or *Giri Bala* in this month's issue of *Modern Review* and that it was a nice story? It talks about how it is more beautiful when people become involved; they smile, make gestures, and look around as they walk rather than when they remain distant like dolls. In our marriages, the husband controls his wife and he behaves the way he likes. The wife in turn reacts to that. But this is a new way. What do you think of this?

Chellamma: It does not appeal to me. When the bull that pulls a cart grows old, there may be a need for another bull. This will apply to the animals. But, it will not suit human beings.

Bharathi: What do you say, Yadhugiri?

Me: I cannot argue as well as you. It is difficult even living with just one husband. The practice you talk about is not acceptable to me. Just because foreigners do it, can we call the practice civilised?

Bharathi: You are repeating what Chellamma said in a different way. Let it be. Today, your mother and Iyer's wife did not take tea. Madame Richard and I noticed that they left their cups untouched under the table. What was the matter?

Me: My mother drinks tea only from a silver tumbler. Moreover, she does not like tea or coffee. My mother will not drink from a cup that has been used by others and is 'not clean'. Bhagyalakshmi Ammal, too, is like her. I don't know whether she likes tea or not.

Bharathi: Is it unclean to drink even from separate cups?

Me: There was a cloth on the table. She does not like that practice. Chellamma drank the tea because of your insistence. Nobody forces Bhagyammal to do anything and neither will she listen.

Bharathi: I assumed that *swadeshis* will take to new customs. But it does not look like it. It may take a little while longer.

Me: When my mother was sick with diarrhoea, Dr Ambu said that coffee will be good for her. We begged her to drink it as if it was medicine. But she refused.

Chellamma: Our practices are the best. You just simply get excited over anything new.

Bharathi: It is going to be eight. Let's go back.

We all got ready to leave.

I stayed in Puducherry for a month. Then I had to go to Bangalore because of a wedding at my mother-in-law's house. On the day I had to leave, I went to Bharathiyar's and Iyer's houses to say goodbye. When I went to his house, Bharathiyar had just finished writing the song *Agni Thomam*. Chellamma and I went upstairs to see him. Bharathiyar sang the song for us, which began with the line 'On the Altar of Our Sacrifice'. He sang one line with great majesty and passion and another line with great sorrow. We were really moved when the demons wept in the poem. Tears started rolling down Chellamma's eyes.

Bharathi: Are you crying because all the diseases are getting eradicated? Lovely!

Chellamma: When you sing, I am not able to control my tears.

Me: Give me this note with the song. Last year, inspectors in Villuppuram took away the draft of your song. What can we do about this?

Bharathi: You better write *Agni Thomam* in bold letters on top. They will leave it alone.

Chellamma: They will not when they see your name on it. Yadhugiri, why don't you copy this song in your notebook? Do not carry this note with you.

Me: I do not have the time to write it down now. I have already written down *Pudhumai Penn* (Modern Woman). I will keep this along with that. As he suggested, I will write *Agni Thomam* in bold letters. Let us see what they do this time.

Bharathi: Do that. If they take it away, do not worry I will send you another copy. Go safely now.

Iyer had finished writing two stories then, *Mangayarkarasi's Love* and *The Peepul Tree by the Pond*. Both were filled with sorrow.

I scolded Nagarajan (the protagonist in the second story) to my heart's content. Iyer said, 'As everyone is happy and satisfied with life, these kinds of stories are beginning to be appreciated'.

I set out the same night. Just as Bharathiyar had said, the inspectors left the note with the song alone.

We Welcome the Devas

I went to Bangalore from Puducherry, then spent four months in Mysore after my marriage, and eventually came to Madras with my grandmother. My mother, who was in Madras, left for Puducherry a few days later. She took the two silver Krishna idols that I had brought from Mysore and gave them to Bharathiyar's second daughter Sakuntala and Iyer's daughter Subhathra. It seems Sakuntala used to play with it all the time, regularly giving it a bath and putting it to sleep. Bhagyalakshmi Ammal put her Krishna idol in a small box with a red cloth underneath it and kept it on the puja platform.

I had postal correspondence with Swaminathan Dikshidar's daughter. In one of her letters, she mentioned that Sakuntala had lost her Krishna idol and had a high fever because of it. She conveyed to me Bharathiyar's request to bring another Krishna idol without fail for Sakuntala on my next visit. When my mother visited Puducherry soon after, she took a Krishna idol with her and handed it over to Chellamma.

In the month of Iypasi in Nala year, I went to Puducherry with my infant child. Sakuntala had recovered completely. Iyer and Bharathiyar visited me to inquire about my health. I heard that Bharathiyar was no longer lively, cheerful, or sociable. My mother used to say that whenever Bharathiyar used to come there would always be lots of people around him, attracted by the sheer greatness of his poetry. That was no longer the case. I think this isolation must have affected him in the beginning.

At that time, I was very sick. I could not go outside the house whenever the impulse took me like I was able to do earlier. Yet, a few days after reaching Puducherry, I went to Bharathiyar's house with my child. His vow of silence had just ended that day. I had laid the child on a mat. Watching the movements of the child's hands and legs and listening to its babble, Bharathiyar was in raptures and sang the song *Chinnanchiru Kiliye* (The Little Parrot).

'See Chellamma…the way it prattles on sweetly,' said Bharathiyar.

Chellamma: Yadhugiri, it's been a long time since we watched a child playing. So everything the child does seems new and exciting to him.

Bharathi: We are so happy if the child plays, but cannot bear the thought of it falling ill.

Chellamma: I shudder to think of the suffering we went through last year Yadhugiri. In spite of his bravado now, he was so agitated then and went through such agony. We did not have peace however much we prayed. It was Ambal who saved us.

Bharathi: Now Chellamma is able to talk about it Yadhugiri. Then, she didn't even rest for a moment. With a sad expression all the time, she would plead to God, 'Let me get this fever instead, spare the child'. The responsibility of saving both Chellamma and the child fell to me.

Chellamma: And how! If I did not wash my hands after handling the child, he would not let me go in. He would mix some medicine with water in a vessel and ask me to clean my hands with that. Everything I touch after that would stink of that medicine. He would be adamant and insist on me washing my hands. Meanwhile, the child would keep crying and calling out my name incessantly. I had had enough. Now the whole thing seems like a dream.

Bharathi: If you did not sanitise your hands, how would the germs get killed? The doctor had given strict instructions to do so, but still, Chellamma would not listen after handling the child. That was a deadly viral fever too.

Chellamma: It was the second week of high fever. The child couldn't even open her eyes. Around eight o'clock, he used a thermometer and found that her temperature was high. He shook the thermometer to check again. It slipped from his hands, hit the floor and broke into pieces. My hands were trembling and I was terrified. Not knowing what to do, I sent the servant lady to the doctor's house. The doctor came, examined the child, gave an injection, asked us not to worry and said that she'd be alright in the morning; we just had to see the night through. He also said that it was not safe to entrust us with a thermometer. The child was delirious with fever and couldn't even speak. I sat unmoving like a stone doll by the child. He could not bear to see her like that and cried out hitting his head against the wall, '*Paapa*, I hoped that you would become a learned pandit and give lectures in big forums. Now, you are not able to utter even a word'. I went up to him and consoled him. The whole night he kept crying out, '*Sakthi*, *Sakthi*' without sleeping. The fever went down a little in the morning. Such a severe fever and we had no money. It was unbearable.

Bharathi: We really went through so much suffering during those two months Yadhugiri. It was not this bad when Thangamma had pneumonia; Nanjunda Rao took care of her like his own child. Swarnam was also there. I did not feel so helpless then.

Chellamma: Appadurai[7] was also there, so you were free of any responsibility then. You were happy with your office friends. Now, who is there to help us tide over this?

Me: Meena had written to me. I was worried. Ayya wrote to say that Sakuntala was getting better.

Then I asked how many new songs he had composed and sung.

Chellamma: His vow of silence has taken precedence over the composition of new songs Yadhugiri. Even I could not take it. The man who was talking and singing nonstop turned mute and communicated only by writing, or with signs like a dumb

7 Chellamma's elder brother.

man...I do not know what kind of a fad this is.

Bharathi: Why don't you too try to remain silent once in a while Chellamma. There is an indescribable pleasure in silence.

Chellamma: No thank you, I have enough pleasures. Who will answer the milk, buttermilk, and oil vendors if I take a vow of silence too? I do not know who introduced him to this silence business.

Bharathi: No one told me about it Chellamma. I just happened to do it one day and felt exhilarated. And started doing it regularly. If I stick to the routine three days a week, my writing also goes on uninterrupted and *Swadesamitran* also sends money regularly. Isn't it good for you too?

Chellamma: It is the rainy season now and the roof tiles are all broken. The landlady has asked us to get the repair work done ourselves. My sister-in-law told me that there is a good house for a lower rent at the end of this street. The landlord had come yesterday. But, he was observing his vow of silence. I told the landlord that he would meet him the next day. This kind of abstinence is alright for swamis, sadhus, and mendicants. Is it practical for people with families? Do the scriptures forbid him from writing if he speaks with others? If he wants, let him decide not to speak for four hours. When he observes his vow of silence, nothing gets done in the house. Like everything else, this too is a game for him. Who knows for how long I have to put up with this strange behaviour.

Bharathi: Chellamma, you do not have to feel so frustrated. I have already taken the new house. All we have to do is just move in on an auspicious day. Hereafter, I will undertake a vow of silence only for a few days a month. I want to find a new word like '*Aum*' in Tamil. That is why I have taken up this vow.

Then Bharathiyar sang the song *Thevar Varugavendru* (We Welcome the Devas). He brought the notes that he had jotted down for me.

These were the songs the notes contained, *Sakthikku Athma Samarpanam* (The Soul's Surrender to Sakthi), *Aiyamundu, Baiyamillai Maname* (No Fear Despite Doubts), *Iyarkai Endrunai Uraippar* (They Call You Nature), *Ulagathu Nayagiye Engal Muthumari* (Our Muthumari, Goddess of the World), *Kaalamam Vanathil* (Time in Wilderness), *Pozhudhu Pularndhadhu* (It Has Dawned), *Malargalin Mevu Thiruve* (The Sacred Flower of Your Body), and a section of *Kuyil Paattu* (Cuckoo's Song). I brought them home with me.

Give Me a Patch of Land

On the eighth day of the Karthigai month in the Nala year (15 November 1916), an auspicious Wednesday, Bharathiyar shifted to the new house. People were restless because there had been no rain in the month of Iypasi that year. But in the month of Karthigai, there were heavy rains and cyclones.

On the day Bharathiyar shifted to the new house, dark clouds had been gathering since four o'clock in the evening. Our house was comfortable to live in during the summer, but not in the rainy season. The rain would spray right into most of the living spaces. Except for the room facing the street, the lower level room between the stairs and the space with the swing, the rest of the house would get flooded.

We had our dinner by seven o'clock and went upstairs while my mother remained downstairs. There were two benches. My two sisters, my father and I, with my child on my lap, were seated on them.

It started raining by eight o'clock. We had read in the *Bhagavata Purana* about Indiran causing a heavy downpour, but now we could see it for ourselves. The loud thunder almost shook the house, lightning pierced through the sky; gusty winds started blowing, making the situation worse. The raindrops were as thick as the little finger.

The wall on one side of the house was very high, built in violation of the rules. It was an old building. There was no landlord, just a landlady who was only interested in collecting the rent and was least interested in getting the house repaired.

Each time it thundered, the house seemed to shake to its foundations. The wall on the eastern side had a glass window. Around midnight, the wall collapsed.

We all took refuge near the western side wall, terrified that it might fall on our heads anytime. My father said, 'If this big wall falls, we would all get crushed beyond recognition. But, by Perumal's grace, that will not happen'.

We were terrified to think of what might have happened to my mother downstairs. The gale made it impossible even to hear what the person next to you was saying. We realised that the wall in the backyard had also collapsed. We were in a state of terror throughout the night.

After five o'clock in the morning, the cyclone began to weaken gradually. When it finally subsided, we looked around the house and saw that things like the clock and framed photographs had all fallen and shattered to pieces.

When we stepped out after six o'clock, our flooded street looked like a river. The gutter a furlong away from our house was overflowing and the sewage had mingled with the rainwater flowing along the street. There were fallen trees everywhere. Even the coconut and portia trees had been uprooted. Fallen electric poles and severed wires were all over the place.

When we came downstairs in the morning, my mother's first question was whether we were all still alive.

Iyer and Bharathiyar came by around 6:30 am and comforted us. 'Are you all safe? It does not matter if your belongings are lost or destroyed. It is enough that you are all alive.' They left after talking to us for some time.

Iyer called me and said, 'Yadhugiri, clean the house as much as possible and attend to the cooking. The plight of the poor in the town must be really bad. We will give them whatever assistance we can. Ask your mother not to go out for a bath. There are corpses floating around. This is only a temporary situation and when it is over she can bathe in the pond. Remain indoors'.

We all stayed inside the house as instructed. But my mother insisted on going to the sea or a pond for a bath. People on the street told her, 'Think this flooded street is the pond, take bath here itself and go home. You cannot walk in the streets because there are countless fallen trees all over. It is difficult to even find the pond'. But my mother was adamant, ignored all the advice, went to the pond, had a bath, and returned home around twelve in the afternoon.

Some *swadeshis* pooled their money and sent Nagasamy and four or five others to collect more money from the public. They retrieved the bodies from damaged huts, performed the last rites for those who lost their lives, got the injured people and those who had lost their homes together, and arranged medical treatment for the injured. They also made arrangements for cooking gruel in the Eswaran Dharmaraja temple for the poor. Other philanthropists in Puducherry also joined in the humanitarian efforts. With the available mud, together they helped build huts for the poor; they made roofs for the huts with the fallen coconut fronds. As a team, they divided the work among themselves, supervised and made sure that no one relaxed or turned lazy till the huts were constructed for those affected.

Even amidst such havoc, Bharathiyar's appreciation of nature remained intact. When he came home the next day, he reported, 'Yadhugiri, a grey-haired old woman approached me as I was learning to weave the coconut fronds. She said, "My house has fallen and has been washed away. I do not have the means and my vision is poor. Do me a favour and build my house. You will be blessed". I asked her to show me her house and she showed me a mere doorframe without a door, roof, or wall around it. I burst out laughing. She responded saying, "If you had seen my house before the cyclone, you would not laugh like this. You would have appreciated its beauty. Now that it has fallen without a trace, you laugh. This body too will meet the same fate one day. All because of this Yaman of a wind". I was struck by remorse. What she said was right. When life departs, only the skeleton remains. I agreed to undertake the work and we all built the house together for her'.

The above incident appeared the next day in Bharathiyar's column in *Swadesamitran.*

'That day I understood the meaning of Sankaracharya's words—When *maya* vanishes, nothing remains. It is merely a frame, either when there is no wind at all or if there is too much wind,' said Bharathiyar.

That day, there was a public announcement saying that it would take at least a month for the water and electricity services to resume and that people, particularly children and women, should remain indoors for a week. That people should get their own lamps ready for use.

The town that used to look like a coconut grove and the streets lined with portia trees became a mere expanse of sand. It took a month for the municipality staff to clear all the fallen branches and trees from the streets.

Sankara Chettiar was frustrated that the municipality wanted to plant new trees. 'If the portia tree branches were cut and planted in a row, they would all grow big in four or five years and the streets would regain the same old look. But the municipality is not listening to anybody and wants to plant new trees. Madness,' he said.

After the huts were all built, the benefactors made arrangements for the poor to go to work. The rain storm had flattened all toddy and arrack shops to the ground. The heavy drinkers had no access to liquor and they were indistinguishable from normal people.

In Eswaran Dharmaraja temple, the poor were served gruel twice a day for a month. The *swadeshis* worked hard, shoulder to shoulder with the labourers throughout the month.

It was only after taking these measures, that steps were taken to get our house repaired. There was a big demand for masons. It took close to three months to build the walls which had collapsed. It was not just our house that needed large-scale repairs. Almost the whole of Puducherry had become a wilderness. Yet, Bharathiyar never lost his sense of humour and mischievousness. He would imitate the sound of rainfall and sing the song *Thikkuhal Ettum Sidhari* (Scattered in All Directions) accompanied by dramatic gestures.

After attending to all the urgent repair work, Bharathiyar went on a round to see the ponds and groves he used to haunt before. There was a small grove with not more than a hundred coconut trees. Except for a few, the rest were still standing. On seeing that, he wanted to sing in praise of Parasakthi who had saved the poor man's farm. Immediately he composed a poem called *Pizhaitha Thennanthoppu* (The Grove that Survived the Cyclone).

'Do we need a better illustration to show that even the wind has mercy on the poor?' asked Bharathiyar. The next day, we all went to see that grove. It became an exhibition site after Bharathiyar sang about it. People began to visit the place and were happy to see it had escaped the full wrath of the storm.

That particular day, Japan passed a new law. To make sure that there were no beggars or lazy people in Japan, the country decided to divide the land among all the Japanese people. When *swadeshi* leaders in Puduvai heard about it, they did some research to find out how much land was needed for a small family to survive. Bharathiyar sang about it in the song *Kaani Nilam Vendum* (Give Me a Patch of Land).

Bharathiyar used to say that children, once they were twenty years old, should be on their own; that parents had the duty to support them only till then and that after that they should take care of their own needs and not be a burden to their parents.

We Want Freedom

We were all invited to the special pujas that Chellamma and Bharathiyar had arranged for Parasakthi who had saved us from the cyclone. Meena, her sister-in-law, Meena's mother, Sankara Chettiar's daughter Padmavathy, her daughter Raji, the teacher's wife, Bhagyalakshmi Ammal and I gathered in Bharathiyar's house. When all the pujas got over, Bharathiyar first sang *Vande Matharam* and then his newly composed *Penmai Vaazhgendru* (Hail Womanhood!) in an English tune. Then he wanted each one of us to sing a song, but Meena's mother refused.

Bharathi: Ok, if the elders do not want to sing, let the children sing. None of the men are strangers here. We are your own brothers.

Meena's mother asked her daughter and her daughter-in-law to sing. After the pujas, each of us received the auspicious betel leaves and areca nut and left for home.

Meena's mother: I did not know that you were so mischievous. I belong to the old generation. The men of our times used to speak politely in front of everyone but make fun of us behind our backs. Sorry. That is why I refused.

Bharathi: We are not scoundrels like that. We abhor the subordination and harassment of women.

Meena's mother: Okay. Aren't you thinking of marriage for Thangamma?

Bharathi: I have not thought about it. Let's see.

Meena's mother: In our days, the elders in the family would get restless even when the girl turned eight. Nowadays people do not bother even when they are sixteen. Chellamma, find a good alliance for Thangamma as soon as possible.

Chellamma: Don't we need money ammami? In our place, everyone demands a huge dowry. How to find a suitable boy under these circumstances?

Meena's mother: It is most important to find a suitable boy. Once you do that, money can be arranged somehow. Do not misunderstand me Chellamma. I just said what came to my mind.

Chellamma: You are not wrong ammami. My sister will come from Kasi this year. My Thangamma grew up as her kid. Most probably, my sister will return to Kasi only after finalising Thangamma's marriage.

It seemed to me that something was bothering Chellamma and she wanted to talk about it but was unable to. I could not figure out the reason behind the change in Chellamma and Bharathiyar.

My mother was away on a trip to another town. I did not know how to give an oil bath to my child. Chellamma would come home around four in the evening. I would keep hot water ready and Chellamma would give an oil bath to my child. Then all of us would go to the beach. Bharathiyar, too, would accompany us. But he was not his usual self and would talk to us only if he felt like it. Suddenly some misunderstanding would crop up between him and Chellamma, and Bharathiyar would go and sit on the sand, away from us. He would join us only when we headed back home.

The people from the Siva temple wanted Bharathiyar to compose a song for Sivarathri. He agreed and composed the song *Muruga! Muruga! Muruga!* If twenty people sang that in unison, they would be filled with religious fervour, he said.

Bharathiyar would also sing the ten songs of Nammaazhwar in *Thiruvaimozhi* starting with *Ivaiyum Avaiyum Uvaiyum*,

> *This and that, and these and those,*
> *and all other people, and places, and things,*
> *whatever, whichever, whoever they are, they're all within him.*

(Translated from Tamil by Vasantha Surya)

Bharathiyar would sing the song as if his whole body was enveloped by the spirit of the song. At that time I could not fully understand the meaning of the song. I used to wonder, 'He calls himself a God; what kind of a powerless God was he who could not solve his own problems'. Yet my respect, devotion, and love for Bharathiyar did not reduce one bit.

Bharathiyar was certainly not his old self. There was a change in his behaviour and I feared that somebody was dragging him in the wrong direction. But no one could change his ways. He ignored Chellamma's pleas. I was not a child anymore to discuss issues freely with him like I used to do. I was the mother of a child now. I felt free to talk about anything with Chellamma. But not with Bharathiyar.

Bharathiyar would stare intently at things without blinking. But the spark was missing from his eyes and gaze. Chellamma used to say that his eyes had lost their intensity because they were constantly looking up at the sun.

One day he came home and sang the song *Vendumadi Viduthalai* (We Want Freedom) in the form of a *keerthanai*, a devotional hymn.

Me: Why a *keerthanai*?

Bharathi: Thangamma does not like my old tunes and she wanted it in the form of a *keerthanai*. Is it good?

Me: Yes it is.

Bharathi: Yadhugiri, I am in search of a new path.

Me: What is that?

Bharathi: I do not want to die and I will find a way to prevent it.

Me: One can perform other miracles, but people say it is impossible to conquer death. It will be truly a miracle if you manage to do it.

Bharathi: I am trying. I think I will succeed.

My father, who arrived then said, 'Why tie a palm fruit on the head of a tiny bird.... Why all these philosophical discussions with her Bharathi? Let her figure out all that when she grows older. Now do not bother her with such complex discussions'.

Bharathiyar got up and left without saying a word. I kept singing the song *Vendumadi Viduthalai* that had been scribbled on the note he had given me, over and over again.

Stream

Dr Ambu told me that if I walked on the beach for an hour early in the morning every day, it would be good for my health. I followed his advice, leaving my child with my mother. My father and younger sister would accompany me. I did this for about a month.

When we were walking on the beach early one morning, we heard a lovely song wafting in the air. The sweet and soul-stirring song was rendered in *Udhaya Ragam*. Listening to it closely, I recognised it as a song from *Thiruvaimozhi*. The voice sounded very familiar and striking, very much like Bharathiyar's. I checked with my father.

Me: Ayya, doesn't it sound like Bharathiyar's voice?

Sri Sri: Come, let's go and find out.

The three of us went in the direction of the song. Bharathiyar was seated on a catamaran there. Black shirt. *Kachchai veshti.* Folded hands. Bharathiyar was facing the sun rising above the ocean and singing. It was still a little dark as the sun had not yet fully risen. The combination of a majestic, resounding voice, an enchanting *raga,* and profound lyrics made us feel that we were seeing God himself right before our eyes. The experience warmed my heart and gave me goosebumps.

Sri Sri: Bharathi, what are you doing here?

Bharathi: Is that you anna? How come you are here so early with the children?

Sri Sri: The doctor advised Yadhugiri to walk on the beach for an hour in the mornings. So for the past few days, we have been walking here from five to six. Yadhugiri thought it sounded like your voice. We followed the song and, sure enough, you are right here singing.

Bharathi: I came here last night. I was adrift in the world of imagination. When I woke up, I found myself here on the beach. The air was cold. I was in ecstasy, singing the *Thiruvaimozhi* song when you called out.

Sri Sri (sounding annoyed)**:** Your family at home will be so worried. What kind of an imaginary world is this? Do you think what you are doing is right?

Bharathi (with a bowed head)**:** The heat is unbearable. The beach and the imaginary world seemed so comfortable. Did Chellamma come to your house and inquire about me? Am I a small child?

My father almost embraced him like his own brother, held both his hands, and got him off the catamaran. He urged us to walk calmly ahead and talked to Bharathiyar in English. Bharathiyar did not respond at all but we found him shedding copious tears. The scene continues to haunt me.

We all went to Bharathiyar's house where Chellamma was waiting at the doorstep. Thangamma and Sakuntala were sleeping. She did not question Bharathiyar about where he had been. The moment she saw my father, she went in, her face lowered. We woke Thangamma and Sakuntala up and then went to our house. My younger sister started questioning my father.

Ranganayaki: Ayya, Bharathiyar's eyes were watering so much. Was he crying? Why?

Sri Sri: The beach sand must have gotten into his eyes.

Me: Ayya, Chellamma didn't even say a word to Bharathiyar although he was not home all night.

Sri Sri: This would not have been the first time. Who knows for how long he has been roaming around at night on the beach or in coconut groves like this?

Me: Ayya, I have been observing him since I came from Madras. Bharathiyar is not his old self at all. The atmosphere in his house seems quite disturbing.

Sri Sri: Do not ask Chellamma or Bharathiyar anything. They will get upset.

Iyer came home that evening. As usual, we went to the beach. I told Iyer what had happened in the morning.

Iyer: Did he respond as soon as Ayya called him?

Me: Yes, he did and was surprised to see us. He regained his composure after we told him about our daily walks on the beach. I do not understand why he is in this state. Ayya does not tell me anything clearly. Chellamma seems terribly upset and is unable to speak about it. It all seems a mystery to me. Why don't you at least tell me what is happening?

Iyer: When a new impulse strikes him, Bharathiyar does not even stop to consider whether it is good or not. I have talked to him many times about it. He pays no heed and proceeds according to his whim. I do not know what danger lies ahead. I don't think the tension in his house will get resolved any time soon. The mistress of a house can perhaps get her way with the children and others but, in our country, can never control or dictate terms to the husband. There are no problems in a household where the head of the family behaves in a just and fair manner. When he errs, the home loses its cheer and is filled with dissatisfaction, rumblings, and tears. The house seems like a prison. The wife cannot reject the husband or abandon the children. When this unhappy situation gets worse, the husband seeks ways in which he can forget domestic troubles.

Ignoring his standing in society and family duties, he starts taking intoxicants to live in the moment, happily lost in the world of imagination. If one consumes drugs, it will help forget one's troubles and build castles in the air. As the effect of the drugs wanes, the body loses its strength and becomes like crushed sugarcane, the juice of life squeezed out of it. If we try to stop an illiterate fool from going to a toddy shop, he would retort, 'I use my money to drink. Who are you to question me?' Still, we can use brute force and stop those fools from drinking for some time. But we cannot restrain weak yet educated men for even a minute. The person who tries to do that is the fool. All we can do is feel wretched. Our advice would likely fall on deaf ears.

Me: The song he sang in *Udhaya Ragam* was very nice.

Iyer: He has an amazing booming voice. It must have been early morning and his singing, mingling with the twittering of birds and the roaring of the sea, would have sounded majestic. I can imagine the scene even from the way you describe it. All that is ok. But the company of some sadhus and mendicants is dragging him in a different direction. A strong man is one who controls his mind. The human mind can, like a monkey, leap from one desire to another, but going down that path is neither good for the person nor those close to him. The lives of people can get destroyed like this.

Upon saying this, Iyer heaved a big sigh. I could not understand anything. I was thoroughly confused.

The Boon of Immortality

In the Pingala year, 1917, a series of events occurred. None of them happy, though.

My father sent me a letter from Puducherry saying that my mother had given birth to a boy. As there was no one to help them in the house, he wanted me to come home. I set out immediately. I halted in Bangalore on the way and stayed in my uncle's house. Unexpectedly, my child became sick and died there.

I was grief-stricken and reached Puducherry, only to hear more sad news. Meena had lost her child during delivery. She was also suffering from health problems. It seems Meena expressed a desire to see me, and Chellamma took me to her house. Meena's condition was pathetic. When she saw me she screamed as if possessed, 'Yadhugiri, bring back my child!' After a while, she regained her composure a little and narrated to me, as if telling me a story, the terrible nature of her sickness, all the happenings when I was away, including the loss of her child. I controlled my sorrow and consoled her. 'Meena, doesn't Bharathiyar always tell us that fear is poison and courage the nectar of immortality? Do not be disheartened.' I told her many such comforting words and tried my best to console her but did not succeed. She was repeatedly crying out 'my child, my child'. She frequently went breathless. We were all worried that she might have caught pneumonia.

It was really hard getting away from Meena. I hardened myself and left her house with Chellamma. From there, we went to Chellamma's house. I had controlled myself in front of Meena, but on reaching Bharathiyar's house, I could not bear it anymore and burst out crying. Leaving Meena like that in the shadow of death broke our hearts. Chellamma and I cried inconsolably. Bharathiyar's eyes were also brimming with tears.

Bharathiyar had just begun his fifteen-day vow of silence that day. After a while, he called us upstairs. He wrote and gave me a note with the words, 'It is our misfortune to see you without your child'.

I looked at him closely. He was a mere skeleton! His eyes were bloodshot and he was weak. I could not bear to see him like that.

As if sensing what was going through my mind, he wrote, 'I am pursuing a new path, doing penance. So I have gone thin'.

He had just finished writing the disrobing section in *Panchali Sabatham* that day. He sang that section for us. On days when he observed silence, he would not speak but would sing his poems.

Chellamma said sadly, 'Yadhugiri, till now we have only watched fate play its game. But look at the game we play with our own actions. If God destroys half the life of a man, should he destroy the other half? It breaks my heart to see the man who used to sing "My voice will not remain useless even for a second," gesture like a dumb man. I do not understand this fate nor his ways. Such hardship should not befall even our enemy. I cannot bear to see him like this'.

Bharathiyar wrote, 'If I observe silence to discover the right word, Chellamma makes fun of me'.

I sat there quietly for some time. Chellamma made me eat and also had some food herself. Then we all went upstairs and resumed our conversation.

Me: Chellamma, will Meena survive?

Chellamma: I will be surprised if she lives beyond two days…

Me: Hm! Some time ago, Bharathiyar talked about finding a path to immortality. My father interrupted and changed the subject. I remembered those words of Bharathiyar even when my child died in Bangalore. Death is terrible. Will he not save Meena from death?

Bharathiyar tried to write something. On seeing that, Chellamma got up abruptly, took my hand and led me downstairs. She took leave of me saying, 'Yadhugiri, do not bring up that subject with him. It is getting late. It is better you get back home'.

The songs Bharathiyar sang about women's freedom were only that, just words. He made Chellamma do whatever he wanted. Chellamma could rarely follow her own desires.

However much Chellamma objected, Bharathiyar continued to observe silence for months together. Once he went forty days without speaking and composed many poems. Those poems are now being circulated under the title, *Bharathi Arubathaaru* (*Bharathi 66*). When we read the poems now, we can understand what he must have gone through then to write them.

After a few days, Sivakami Ammal and Subramania Siva came to Puducherry bearing the flag of Mother India. Since they came straight to Bharathiyar's house, he was forced to give up his vow of silence and talk to them. They had come to our house after visiting Aurobindo Ghosh and Iyer. Appa told me that as it was past twelve, they had stood outside, talked with him and left.

This God

One day, when I went to Bharathiyar's house, Chellamma was arguing with Bharathiyar about something. The moment she saw me, she complained sadly, 'Look here Yadhugiri… isn't he a Brahmin? Isn't it shameful that he keeps his daughter unmarried in the house? Not only that, he goes around sharing domestic matters with everyone in town. Shouldn't we be discreet at least with society? How can I face people now? What will my parents think of me?'

Bharathi: Yadhugiri, you have come at an interesting time. Come, sit. Chellamma is ranting as if we are witnessing the end of the world. I am not a Brahmin at all. I do not wear the sacred thread, and I do not perform the *sandhya vandhanam* (evening prayer) or make ceremonial offerings to my ancestors. I am a Sudra. The man of the house is a Sudra; the woman of the house is a Brahmin! Have you seen this anywhere? I am like you. So what?

Chellamma: Just because you do not observe rituals, it does not mean that we also shouldn't.

Bharathi: Chellamma, do you perform the *aupasanam* every day? Do you perform the *agni hothram* (fire puja) every day? Do you pray, meditate, observe penance, etc. regularly? How many orphans do you feed? Do the gods come and receive their due (*havirbhagam)* in person? You observe the rituals blindly. It is a hundred years since the rituals became irrelevant. But the practices still continue. They too will disappear in another twenty years!

Chellamma: Now you are making fun of me. You are listing the things that you are supposed to do. Have I ever stopped you from doing these things?

Bharathiyar: There you come around. Will you listen to me quietly without interrupting? Your anger will subside a little if you understand the rationale behind these.

'In Vedic times, people were eating fruits and edible roots. Women did not have much work to do. All that they had to do was sweep, tidy up the house, and fetch water. It was believed that the *devatas* would come directly to receive their due, so women had to stay in an outhouse during menstruation. Unlike women now, they would take a bath even during menstruation. When men are not around, they would bathe in the pond, wash, dry their clothes, and then go to their outhouses. Only infants were allowed to stay with them. During that time, it was important for women to get enough rest. Since they could not fulfil other functions, they were kept away from their husbands.

During such days, if some important arguments broke out between the husband and the wife, they would do it with a screen in between.

'Later, Brahmin women had to do everything on their own, from pounding rice to cooking to serving food. If people from other communities did the work for them, it was considered pollution. Doing difficult tasks like pounding, grinding, or polishing rice, during the days of menstruation was risky. So even if they were Brahmin women, they were kept apart in the outhouse during those days.

'As time went on, there were no ponds in big cities to bathe in. So, during those three days, the women were kept in a small room where they would sweat profusely. Usually, there were people to help with household work. If not, the men themselves would cook food. They never used to go and eat in hotels as the men are doing now. Now all those practices are gone. All the work is carried out by Sudras. Brahmins just buy and eat food from outside. And they create new customs like *kiraya shuddi*. Women do not undertake difficult tasks now. They just cook directly what is bought from the shops. The families are also very small nowadays. If the wife has her periods and is staying in the outhouse, the rice cooked by a servant maid in a hotel is acceptable. But that same servant maid is not allowed to enter the kitchen. There are so many other pollutions in hotel food. But Brahmins are happy if the food is served by someone smeared with holy ash.

'Brahmin women attain puberty earlier than women of other communities. Earlier, even though they may have gotten married at seven, they would not attain puberty till they were sixteen or eighteen. In such marriages, there would not have been a big age difference between the boy and the girl. It is not so now. Nobody questions a man whatever his age may be. Restrictions are laid only for women. If there are restrictions, it should be for both. It takes usually twenty to twenty-five years for boys to complete their studies and become self-reliant. The right kind of match for such boys would be girls aged eighteen or twenty.

'We live in the British Raj and do the work of slaves. When we return home after work, our attention will be on the dinner and not on prayers, penance, and pujas. Rituals are a show put on for others. I do not like them. I did announce with fanfare when my Thangam attained puberty. I will find a suitable husband for her when the time for marriage comes. I have not imprisoned Thangam. Let her live like a princess. She need not come to the kitchen or the puja room if she does not like it.

'It is always good to have a bath in running water. But here we have only tap water. Let her take bath as she usually does on those three days. It is foolish to lock herself up in a small room and make her sweat for three days. You fill warm water for her in a different tub. It is a pleasure to have a bath, be clean, and wear new clothes. But it is important that you do not go for long walks during this time, nor lift heavy objects. That can be risky. Your actions seem to ignore what is important; you fear the skin shed by the snake more than the snake itself. Customs and rituals have become important but meaningless.'

Chellamma: Yesterday you turned the house upside down by shaving yourself. You polluted the house more than once.

Bharathi: Crazy woman…in those days, barbers used to cut up dead bodies. But that was the first step in medical education. Now barbers do not touch the corpses at all. It is now the high-caste Brahmin boy who cuts a corpse as the first lesson in medical studies. A real worker does not care about pollution. Only shirkers care. The marriage customs of Komuttis, Mudaliars, and Naidus have changed according to changing times. It is the Brahmin marriage customs that are still stuck in the dark ages. The day we throw these superstitions aside, we can claim that our country has become three-fourths civilised.

Chellamma: But is it wrong or superstitious to have baths in ponds?

Bharathi: It is good to have a bath by dipping oneself in good, clean ponds. It is good to stay in cold water for a few hours after periods, on the fourth day. It reduces one's body heat. There is a logic behind our elders advising us to have a certain number of dips while taking bath. But now in cities, we do not have clean ponds or springs. It is better to bathe in tap water than bathe in dirty pond water and fall sick. White people fill a broad tub with water and stay in the water for a while. We too could do that. We need good ponds in this town. Then you can have a bath there by all means. Yadhugiri, how is your younger brother, the strong man?

Me: My brother is keeping well. But I do not quite get what you mean.

Bharathi: Chellamma told me that your brother was born during the cyclone. So I call him "the son of the wind, the strong man!"

Me: Like you said, let him remain a strong man of the wind for a hundred years. He is doing quite well.

Bharathi: Don't keep crying all the time thinking of your child Yadhugiri. Plead with Sakthi. Have a bath early in the morning and pray to Sakthi. It'll do you good. Do not lament like an old woman at this young age. What is the use of having read the *Gita*? Pleading with God and getting back what was taken from you is real fortitude. Lamenting is the way of the weak. You have the right to turn around and tell me "You'll understand only if you experience it." But it is not good to pine and wither away. You should strengthen your resolve.

Chellamma: You are all men. *Gita* and *Vedanta* will not help a traumatised mother. However much she prays to Sakthi, can she get her child back? Will the grief go away?

Bharathi: We have to do just our duty, follow the path shown by God, and strengthen ourselves. We should do our best until something goes out of our hands. Once it goes out of our hands, we should just let it go. To give in to grief and give up is foolishness. Crying will do you good when you are grief-stricken. But it is wrong to cry all the time and kill the joy you have in life. 'In sorrow, look up to people better placed in life than you and strive. In financial matters, look at those who are below you and console yourself,' is a wise saying that should be printed in gold.

'Some people go through countless difficulties and grief even at a young age. Some others experience the same in old age. Trust me, from now on, Yadhugiri will emerge victorious in whatever she takes up. Do not keep pining for what is gone. Pray to Sakthi and look forward to all the good that awaits you.'

Then he gave me the script of the song he had composed on the day Thangamma attained puberty and sang it for us.

This Deity is ours!
We're blessed!
There's no room any more
for fear!

Delving deep
Into the holy chants,
you shall know God
reigns over the universe.
You'll be aware, at last
that it's this very Deity
that is your destiny.

Deep in the ground
is the root that feeds
the tree.
Within the womb is found
whatever meets
the embryo's need.
Laws there are
to fit each eventuality.
In Nature's power
resides the key
to immortality.

The world is the body.
Within, the life
that God displays.

Like the light of the sky
this revelation shall spread
everywhere.

All deeds are God's doing.
Every thought is His.

Chanting the Name that bestows
deliverance, the gods awaken
to life.

No disease, no poverty
No agony at losing the thread
that ritual has wound
around us.

As mother, father, friend
God empowers, and bestows
all triumphs.

Fear is gone, and we're no longer
deluded! Love and joy and virtue
are here, and nothing's left
of the dregs of all our past miseries.
Victory is certain! It will soon be!

(*This God*, translated from Tamil by Vasantha Surya)

Editor's note: This song has not appeared in any of Bharathiyar's collections of poetry or essays published so far.

Lecture

In the Chithirai month of Kalayukthi year, on a Friday, Bharathiyar had arranged for a small meeting in his house. He had also invited a few of his women acquaintances.

Bharathiyar started the meeting with his song, *Vande Matharam* and that was followed by *Pengal Vidudhalai* (Women's Freedom) *kummi*. Then he wanted us to speak on whatever subject we wished to talk about. I gave a short speech on the fruits of hard work. Bharathiyar published it in *Swadesamitran* along with his comments.

In those days, we used to get only English newspapers in our homes but not Tamil newspapers. *Swadesamitran* used to be delivered to our family friend, O.M. Parthasarathy Iyengar's house, who was a judge. It seems that the women of his house, on reading my essay, complained loudly to my grandmother that it was the end of the world. It seems the topic was discussed wherever our community people gathered in Thiruvallikeni too.

The next week, Thiruvalluvar day was celebrated in Iyer's house. The poor were fed. Chellamma and Bhagyalakshmi Ammal took charge of the cooking. Iyer narrated certain parts of Thiruvalluvar's life story. As usual, Bharathiyar sang a few songs. I spoke on the matter of 'Women's progress'. I used some of Gandhi's ideas on Satyagraha, quoted some of his statements and pointed out how women themselves acted as barriers to their own progress. The elderly grandmothers were furious with me.

My father now tells me that my speech has been published in Bharathiyar's collection of essays.

When my speeches were published twice in the magazine, my grandmother, older aunt, and second aunt's daughter visited us together. They said categorically that I should stop giving speeches on social reformation. That they could not face people in Thiruvallikeni because of these speeches. They considered it a sin, argued with my father, and finally managed to put an end to my writing.

When Bharathiyar invited me to the meeting next week, my grandmother and aunt also came with me. This time, instead of me, my aunt gave the talk. She said that women should not learn English and that they belonged in the kitchen doing household work obediently. Bharathiyar intervened, quoted a few sayings on the subject and said that there was nothing wrong with women venturing out. They did not agree with him. They also said that Bharathi should not publish my aunt's speech.

Yet, in his essay the next day, Bharathiyar quoted parts of my aunt's speech without mentioning her name.

Praying at His Feet

Chellamma told me that Murugesam Pillai's son Raja Bahadur was returning home after completing his engineering studies in Paris. War was raging then. The parents had made a number of arrangements to celebrate his return and the successful completion of his studies. They decorated the house like a marriage hall with festoons and buntings. They had invited family members and friends. Everyone from Bharathiyar's house, too, was present. The arrangements were grand and spectacular.

In most matters in life, man proposes one thing and God disposes of it. It happened in Murugesam Pillai's case too. The day he thought would be the happiest in his life turned out to be the saddest. As everyone was in a celebratory mood to welcome Raja Bahadur, it was a telegram that arrived instead of him. It announced that the ship in which Raja Bahadur had been sailing was shelled by German bombs and sunk without a trace.

Murugesam Pillai fainted on reading the telegram. He regained consciousness after a long time, but the man who fell down never stood up after that. The news that broke his heart broke him physically too. He cried, screamed, lamented, and ranted. He could not be pacified despite the attempts of many to console him.

Bharathiyar was seated next to Murugesam Pillai. He compared Murugesam Pillai's state of mind to Dasarathan's. As he continued to cry, Murugesam Pillai kept repeating details about Raja Bahadur's childhood—the way he crawled, the way he mouthed meaningless words as a baby, his sharp brain, and so on. An elder had once said that if a pregnant woman exposed herself to sunlight, the foetus would grow to be a strong child. When Murugesam Pillai heard this, he used to make his wife sit for one hour every day on a bench in the sun, ignoring the objections of others. His wife kept mentioning this while crying inconsolably.

Bharathiyar tried his best to console the couple. He sang for them the heart-rending songs of Mandodhari's lament on the death of Indrajithan in *Kambaramayanam*, the lament of Dasarathan in Kulasekara Alwar's song *Van Thaalinai Vanangi* (Praying at His Feet) and Devaki's lament *Aladhan Karumbannavan Thalo.* The couple kept quiet, listening for a while and then started lamenting again. Murugesam Pillai was already afflicted with some disease. This terrible loss made it worse and the medical treatment he was undergoing became ineffective. The doctor said that there was very little hope of him surviving. Murugesam Pillai kept constantly asking, 'Has Raja Bahadur arrived?'
Murugesam Pillai's friends got together and decided that Murugesam Pillai should have some peace at least in death. They

made Aurobindo Ghosh take a fake telegram to Murugesam Pillai stating that Raja Bahadur had escaped the German attack and would arrive the succeeding week. Aurobindo Ghosh never used to leave his house, but, considering Murugesam Pillai's pathetic condition, agreed to do what he could. Murugesam Pillai listened to Aurobindo Ghosh quietly but refused to believe him. 'The telegram may be a real one. But I cannot bring myself to believe its content. What was within grasp, has gone beyond reach now. I do not know how to repay you for all the trouble you have taken to bring me comfort.'

When this attempt failed, his friends tried other ways. They dressed a man who looked a little like Raja Bahadur in western clothes and took him to Murugesam Pillai. 'See, Raja Bahadur has come straight from the ship.' Murugesam Pillai had already lost his ability to speak. He opened his eyes wide and peered at the man intently. With an expression of distrust and disgust, he turned his back to them. In a few minutes, his tormented soul left his body.

As if to prove the words of the elders right and as though God had responded to the pleas of Murugesam Pillai, exactly on the twenty-seventh day after he died, Raja Bahadur arrived safely. It seems he held on to a floating wooden block of the sunken ship, swam to a sandbank, and took another passing ship. People there sorrowfully welcomed him. They told him about Murugesam Pillai's last moments.

Bharathiyar wondered, 'Murugesam Pillai gave up his life for the sake of his son. If he had been alive, would the son have returned?'

The Exit

When I was in Puduvai, Chellamma had gone to her native place Kadayam to help with the arrangements for her younger brother's marriage. Bharathiyar was under a vow of silence for the entire month she was away. He never came to my house. I, too, could not go to his house like I used to earlier.

Within a few days after Chellamma returned, she got a telegram announcing the death of her father. Chellamma went to Kadayam again, leaving her children Thangamma and Sakuntala in Puduvai. They would come to our house and play with us.

Chellamma returned from Kadayam in a few days. Following her return, she spoke of wanting to leave Puducherry for good and going back to British India. Her relatives also urged her to give up the hardships of living in a strange place and asked her to return to her own town. Bharathiyar, too, was fed up with Puducherry. But there were many risks involved in his return to British India.

His relatives had made Bharathiyar's brother and sister write to him, urging him to leave Puducherry. But Bharathiyar ignored the letters. Not wanting to leave Bharathiyar alone, Chellamma too had come to terms with living there.

Chellamma had come to see my child in the month of Purattasi. 'It is not possible to live here anymore. We will shift to Kadayam,' she said. But she did not speak about how it was possible. We knew that Bharathiyar would not leave Puducherry because he would be arrested and imprisoned if he went out of town.

Bharathiyar told us the next morning that when he was upstairs, Chellamma had prepared to leave with the children for Kadayam, only carrying some essential things. That she insisted on leaving despite him asking her not to, that he was planning to marry again.

But Chellamma came back in a week with her brother Appadurai.

Around the fifteenth of the month of Iypasi, Bharathiyar, Chellamma, and Appadurai went to a place near Villianur. As soon as they crossed Villianur, the police arrested Bharathiyar and put him in Cuddalore jail.[8]

Chellamma and Appadurai returned to Puducherry, vacated the house, settled all their accounts, and went to Kadayam with the children.

8 On 20 November 1918, Bharathiyar set out of Puducherry with his family. He was arrested the same day. He was released on December 14, after twenty-four days in jail.

Bharathiyar was released from the jail in Cuddalore after a few days. He came straight to our house and stayed with us for a few days. During that time, he also gave a few lectures on the beach in Chennai.

Some of his relatives tried to arrange a separate house for him in Kadayam, tried to make him stay there and change his ways. But nothing worked.

After that, I had no information or news about Bharathiyar for about one and a half years. I would keep reading *Swadesamitran* to see if there was an essay or article written by him, but there was no news of him whatsoever.

The End

My father and Iyer came from Puduvai in the month of Chithirai, in the Roudri year (1920). They too found their freedom when the war ended. My father had decided to stay in Puduvai until Iyer also was released from prison. Upon his release, both of them left Puduvai. Aurobindo Ghosh was the only one who stayed back there.

For a few days, 'The Puduvai Three'—Bharathiyar, Iyer, and Aachariyar (my father)—got to live again in the same town, Chennai. Bharathiyar worked in the *Swadesamitran* office and Iyer in the *Desa Bakthan* office. My father resumed his old business.

I had come from Mysore to Chennai towards the end of the Iypasi month. Chellamma and Iyer's wife Bhagyalakshmi Ammal came to see me. I remember vaguely that Iyer was living in George Town. Bharathiyar was living on Thulasinga Perumal Koil Street in Tiruvallikeni. Our house was on Peyyalvar Koil

Street, on the northern side of the temple, opposite its front entrance *mandapam*.

Bharathiyar would be in his house only from seven to nine in the morning and would then leave for his office. On some days, he would come home in between office hours.

The promotion of Hindi in Chennai had just begun then. Mahatma Gandhi's son, Devdas Gandhi, used to teach Hindi and the singing of patriotic songs in our house upstairs. Bharathiyar, who knew Hindi well, would also participate. When a three-month-old child would shake its hands and legs and make a noise that sounded like 'Aav, aav', Bharathiyar would sing, 'Aavo, aavo, aavo Sahala Bharatha Kumar! The little child wants us all to be united. We are foolish and do not pay heed'.

The political situation in the country then was turbulent. The Ali brothers had been arrested when they were on their way to Chennai. Their mother, a brave woman, came to Chennai and addressed a public meeting on the beach. After her speech, when the crowd was about to disperse, Bharathiyar went on to the stage and began to sing, *Jaya Paerigai Kottada* (Beat the Victory Drum). The crowd regrouped again, with many more joining in. The people of that time were crazy about Bharathiyar's songs and speeches. There was such a magnetic appeal in his voice and songs. That day, Bharathiyar then mimicked the drum beat to accompany his singing and made the crowd rapturous.

***

During my visits to Chennai, I would sometimes say in the course of our conversation, 'Both my children are girls. And I lost the only male child I had'. If that ever fell on Bharathiyar's ears, he would say, 'Yadhugiri, girls certainly are more affectionate than boys. You treat me in the same affectionate way you did when you used to play with me in Puducherry. But your brother Sami is consumed with domestic concerns. He has no time to even talk to me'.

I was in Chennai until Ugadi. Bharathiyar used to visit our house every day. Chellamma, Thangamma, and Sakuntala used to visit us often. We too would go to their house frequently.

In the month of Chithirai, Bharathiyar came home in the morning on the day I was leaving. After inquiring about everybody, he shaved himself at the entrance of our house. 'Chellamma said it was not a good day for shaving and would not let me do it in the house so I did it here,' he said.

Bharathiyar came again at six in the evening that day. I took his blessings and asked whether he had plans to visit Bangalore. 'What business do I have in Bangalore, amma? Travel safely. Who knows whether I'll be in this town or some other town when you come here next. That's why I wanted to see you one more time,' he said. That was the last time I saw him.

I was in Mysore when I received a letter from my mother with the news that Bharathiyar was no more. At first, I could not believe it. Then my father confirmed it in a more detailed letter.

Fate had dealt its card. And it was an unfortunate loss for all of Tamil Nadu.

***

In 1923, I visited Chennai again. Chellamma, Thangamma, and Sakuntala came to see me. I felt sad when I met them.

Chellamma said, 'Yadhugiri, he enquired about you even just before he took his last breath. "Where is Yadhugiri?" I told him that you were in Mysore.'

'He asked, "How many children does she have?" Two, just like us, I said.'

'He told me that he had the urge to see you and asked me, "When will she come here? Let her be happy wherever she is. Finish the cooking early tomorrow morning since I have to go to the office by eight," he said. Within an hour of saying this, he was no more. What will I do now? Life is an absurd game.'

***

Today, the mansion of our freedom shines bright, but it is built on the foundation laid by freedom fighters such as Thilagar, Bharathiyar, Chidambaram Pillai, and Va.Ve.Su. Iyer and the countless hardships and difficulties they faced.

Bharathiyar was impelled by an inexplicable force. When he sang, poetry would pour forth spontaneously without any interruption. Sometimes he would be surprised by his own poetic compositions. He never had to struggle to find the right word, rhyme, grammar, or metre. Bharathiyar was a rare gift, a natural poet.

Bharathiyar used to ask himself a number of questions. Sometimes, even I was astonished by that. Once, when I asked him with whom he was talking on the ocean shore, he smiled and said he was talking with Parasakthi. I never understood his words then.

Bharathiyar is an example of how a man should mentally prepare himself and how austere his life should be in order to write beautiful poetry. Such poets are born only once in centuries. The society that has given birth to such geniuses is indeed a blessed one.

The End

Appendix

Bharathiyar's Experience of Nature (Extended Chapter)

M. K. Yadhugiri

It is true that Bharathiyar was a little unhappy that the Tamil people had still not opened their eyes to the world or woken up to the significance of the soul-stirring songs that he had sung to inspire them. But he was very confident that his songs would resound very soon all over Tamil Nadu. It is this strong self-belief that sustained his enthusiasm and kept him going despite all the difficulties he faced. He continued to express his unique feelings through his powerful little songs.

When something in nature appealed to his heart, he would forget all about his domestic troubles and immerse himself in the experience. He would then sing, dance, and rejoice like children would. There would be no place in his heart for worry or care.

His wife Chellamma would find it very difficult in such situations though she would do her best to make his life comfortable. At times, even her patience would run out. If she tried to explain a difficult situation at home, he would crack jokes, laugh like a child and cheer her up.

One Friday evening, Swaminathan Dikshidar's daughter Meena and I went to Bharathiyar's house in Eswaran Dharmaraja Temple Street. Chellamma was not her usual lively, cheerful self. We chatted amongst ourselves as usual, but Chellamma remained withdrawn. At six o'clock, Meena went back home; Chellamma and I were the only ones in the house. We remained silent for a while and then I went and lay my head on her lap and, after five minutes, asked her, 'Chellamma, aren't you well? You do not look like your usual self'.

Chellamma: Nothing is physically wrong with me, Yadhugiri. But I feel as if a worm is gnawing at my mind. I have to unburden myself by sharing it with someone. But you are only a child… what is the use of telling you all this?

Me: It is alright…. Tell me what is bothering you. I'll tell Bharathiyar that this is no way to treat a woman in the house when he is preaching women's liberation to society.

Chellamma: Ayyo, child! You will not understand. It is the end of the month now. We have not yet paid the milkman last month's dues. He asked me yesterday and I told him that I would pay him next month. He refused and insisted on the payment, but somehow I pacified him.

'See, he is supposed to send an article to *Swadesamitran* today but he has not sent it yet. How will they pay him money?

'After his bath, coffee and the routine betel leaves, I talked to him at length. Even put the paper, pen, and ink bottle on the table. But he could not bring himself to write. After cleaning the rice, I went in to change. By the time I came out, he had taken a handful of rice and strewn it in the courtyard and was singing joyfully even as he watched the sparrows pecking at them.

'I came out to collect the rice and found that a quarter of it was gone. I could not control my tears. I was stunned. Seeing this he said, "Chellamma, look at these sparrows! How happy they are! Why can't we be like that? You are constantly arguing with me and I keep yelling at you. These sparrows are teaching us the value of harmony. But, we close our eyes and pay no attention to them. Can we get more stupid than this?"

'I could not bear it anymore and blurted out, "Why are you infuriating me? I wanted to get done with the cooking before the children returned from sister-in-law's (Murugesam Pillai's wife) house. I had cleaned the rice and lighted the fire...only to find that you had thrown the rice to the sparrows! It will take me ten more minutes to clean the rice again. Who knows how long it will be before you get any money? You have not even begun to write the article. The milkman's demands are humiliating. The housemaid has not turned up for two days. Don't you have to think about all these things? And you want me to be happy like these sparrows. God is blind. Otherwise, he would not torture me like this," I said and went back inside.

'When I came out after some time, he was singing the song *Breaking Free* to Sakuntala. The child was jumping with joy. Thangamma was sitting quietly on one side. He was totally lost in the joy of singing. The sparrows were pecking at the rice.

'When everyone is so happy, why should I disturb the peace in the house? So, I too sat down there with them. It was noon by the time the singing and dancing got over.

'"I am hungry. Let's go and eat, appa," said Sakuntala. He, too, settled down to eat without a word. Then turning to me, he said, "Chellamma, are you still angry? Look here, I am going to send this poem about the sparrows. You'll receive the payment on the first day of the month. Don't worry."

'He is a good man, devoid of deceit and ill will. It is not a problem if we have the money in hand. But will the publisher send us money if he does not submit an article on time? That is my only grouse.'

When Chellamma said that, I did not know what to say. What can I say? But just to comfort her, I said calmly, 'A cover has been sent by post today. What if it is a song or an essay?'

Chellamma: Well…you are just his kind of person. You will endorse everything he docs. But I feel a little relief, having shared this with you. That is enough for me.

Just then Bharathiyar came back to the house. Turning to me, he said, 'Yadhugiri, I composed a new song today. Have you seen it?'

'No, but Chellamma told me about it. Show it to me.'

Taking a sheet of paper from the table, he said, 'Chellamma will not like what I am going to say now. Whether I am around to see it or not, Yadhugiri, you will certainly live to see how much these songs of mine are appreciated and celebrated by all. Tamil Nadu is like a baby which has not even opened its eyes yet. Even if it has, it is still in its infant stage. Here, take this song...'

Sparrow Set Free
Like a caged bird set free
unhindered shall you be.
Soaring in the eight directions
afloat upon the buoyant air
that gives of itself, without stint,
to everything, everywhere.
you shall drink the honeyed light
of the Sky.

With your mate you'll revel
in the joy of song and play,
build a nest where misery
shall never dwell,
where eggs will yield
chicks to love and cherish,
tend and nourish
with grain you fetch
from yard and field

Night falls.
You lull them with stories,
and wake them at dawn,
with a song.

(Translated from Tamil by Vasantha Surya)

I remember the poem like this. But now, in his recently published book, the last line is a little different. He might have changed it later.

Just as Bharathiyar said, the Tamil world is in an infant stage, crawling and playing, having opened its eyes. It still has not gained the ability to look around on all four sides. Now we understand clearly the significance of what Bharathiyar said a quarter century ago.

This is the fate of prophets. They sacrifice themselves for the sake of truth that will only be understood in the future. They do not worry about it and happily accept it as the law of nature. Not realising this, we get upset to see them in a state that actually gives them joy. This small difference in mindset is what differentiates ordinary people from the great.

Ananda Vikatan
04/06/1936

Ka. Na. Su's review in *Swadesamitran*

Pudhumaipithan and I were conversing with an elderly friend one day. As he too was a writer, our discussion was naturally about literature. We talked about classic and contemporary literature. I don't remember whether it was So. Ve. or me who asked our friend whether he had ever seen Bharathiyar. He said that he had seen Bharathiyar once or twice from a distance but never had the opportunity to meet him or get to know him personally. A month later, he started publishing dramatic and poetic anecdotes about his meetings and interactions with Bharathiyar in a magazine that was becoming popular then. I vaguely remember that he had serialised his accounts for about twenty to twenty-five weeks.

As Bharathiyar had lived in the recent past, and because many have manufactured memories of him and have made up meaningless folk songs to get appreciated, it is really important that we review and double-check accounts about Bharathiyar before accepting these as true. It is an apt punishment for Bharathiyar, a true poet, to have been born at a time when there was hardly any ray of truth in the hearts of people.

I am not saying that there are no authentic books of reminiscences, truthful in spirit and words. To my knowledge, Va. Ra.'s *Bharathiyar Charithram*, Chellammal's *Dhavapudalvar Bharathiyar* and Yadhugiri Ammal's *Bharathi Ninaivugal* seem to be the better ones. It is quite possible that there are many more books on Bharathi that I am not aware of. Of the three well-written books mentioned above, Yadhugiri Ammal's *Bharathi Ninaivugal* does not cover the entire life of Bharathi. But it brings alive the events of about six to seven years in Bharathiyar's life. Getting to know any poet as an actual living person is indeed a difficult task. It is quite usual for poets to make life very difficult for those who are very close to them. It is not that easy to get to know and understand a poet's longings, desires, or his soul's stirrings. The standard explanations that common people have for different behaviour need not necessarily apply to a poet's actions.

The English writer Samuel Johnson is not considered a great writer today. But *Life of Johnson,* written by James Boswell, is considered one of the best examples of what a good biography ought to be. Boswell has achieved what no other biographer has managed to achieve until now. It was not merely the love that he had for Johnson that made it possible; there was a remarkable likeness and unity of mind that made it impossible to tell one from the other.

Yadhugiri Ammal is the eldest daughter of Mandayam Sri Srinivasaachariyar, who was a close friend and a pillar of support for Mahakavi Bharathiyar. She was a young girl when Bharathiyar was living in Puduvai. She had the privilege of being a close friend of Bharathiyar for many years and became the object of his affection. She has described Bharathiyar as she knew him as a young girl, and we enjoy Bharathiyar through a young girl's perspective. How easily children understand and speak about many truths that the elders struggle to articulate! [An extensive quote from 'Stream' (Chapter 20) follows...]

Me: *Ayya, Chellamma didn't even say a word to Bharathiyar although he was not home all night.*

Sri Sri: *This wouldn't have been the first time. Who knows for how long he has been roaming around at night on the beach or in coconut groves like this?*

Me: *Ayya, I have been observing him since I came from Madras. Bharathiyar is not his old self at all. The atmosphere in his house seems quite disturbing.*

Sri Sri: *Don't ask Chellamma or Bharathiyar anything. They will get upset.*

Iyer came home that evening. As usual, we went to the beach. I told Iyer what had happened in the morning.

Iyer: *Did he respond as soon as Ayya called him?*

Me: *Yes, he did and was surprised to see us. He regained his composure after we told him about our daily walks on the beach. I do not understand why he is in this state. Ayya does not tell me anything clearly. Chellamma seems terribly upset and is unable to speak about it. It all seems a mystery to me. Why don't you at least tell me what is happening?*

Iyer: *When a new impulse strikes him, Bharathiyar does not even stop to consider whether it is good or not. I have talked to him many times about it. He pays no heed and proceeds according to his whim. I do not know what danger lies ahead. I don't think the tension in his house will get resolved any time soon. The mistress of a house can perhaps get her way with the children and others but, in our country, she can never control or dictate terms to the husband. There are no problems in a household where the head of the family behaves in a just and fair manner. When he errs, the home loses its cheer, and is filled with dissatisfaction, rumblings, and tears. The house seems like a prison. The wife cannot reject the husband or abandon the children. When this unhappy situation gets worse, the husband seeks ways in which he can forget his domestic trouble.*

Ignoring his standing in society and family duties, he starts taking intoxicants to live the moment happily in the world of the imagination. If one consumes drugs, it will help one forget one's troubles and build castles in the air...

I have quoted a big section from her book to illustrate Yadhugiri Ammal's clarity of thought and expression and to highlight her enquiry into understanding Bharathiyar.

We see Bharathiyar as a poet, a social activist, a family man, an irresponsible man, as well as a friend in many places in the book. The writer has explained how Bharathiyar composed *Three Loves* on demand, inspired by the English tune of the band musicians who performed in Pondicherry in front of the Dupleix statue. She has explained to us the context, when and how many of Bharathiyar's songs were composed.

That evening, Bharathiyar, accompanied by his daughter Sakuntala, came by around four. My youngest sister, Ranganayaki, and Sakuntala are of the same age. They started playing together as usual...

Bharathiyar, who was listening to their conversation, burst out laughing. 'Children come here. Both of you talk beautifully like parrots–one is a golden parrot and the other an iron parrot. Who wants to be which one?'

Sakuntala: *Appa, I am the golden parrot and Ranga the iron parrot. Right?*

Ranganayaki: *I am the golden parrot, you can be the iron parrot.*

Sakuntala: *No way. It was my father who asked the question, so I am the golden parrot.*

Ranganayaki: *Come on, do not start a fight now. Both of us are golden parrots!*

Bharathiyar was overwhelmed with joy. He carried Ranga over to my father and told them of their conversation. 'I said something insensitive that could hurt the children. But this child set it right.' After that incident, he always called my younger sister 'golden parrot'.

Ranganayaki: *Am I wrong? Aren't we both fair?*

Bharathi: *You are absolutely right. Both of you are golden parrots.*

Ranganayaki: *Why aren't you carrying Sakuntala?*

Bharathi: *Come Sakuntala! Ranga has made you also a golden parrot!*

There are many anecdotes like these that Yadhugiri Ammal has narrated in detail. In each of these, we can see Bharathi, the man. That is the special feature of this compilation of reminiscences.

Yadhugiri's child passes away. Soon after, when she meets him,

Bharathiyar had just begun his fifteen-day vow of silence that day. After a while, he called us upstairs. He wrote and gave me a note with the words, 'It is our misfortune to see you without your child'.

I looked at him closely. He was a mere skeleton! His eyes were bloodshot and he was weak. I could not bear to see him like that.

As if sensing what was going through my mind, he wrote, 'I am pursuing a new path, doing penance. So I have gone thin'.

He had just finished writing the disrobing section in 'Panchali Sabatham' that day. He sang that section for us. On days when he observed silence, he would not speak but he would sing his poems.

Chellamma said sadly, 'Yadhugiri, till now we have watched fate play its game. But look at the game we play with our own actions. If God destroys half the life of a man, should he destroy the other half? It breaks my heart to see the man who used to sing "My voice will not remain useless even for a second" gesture like a dumb man. I do not understand this fate nor his ways. Such hardship should not

befall even our enemy. I cannot bear to see him like this'.
Bharathiyar wrote, 'If I observe silence to discover the right word, Chellamma makes fun of me'.

The people of Tamil Nadu have contented themselves by just building a memorial for Bharathiyar. They have not taken enough effort to appreciate and enjoy his literary legacy or to understand Bharathi, the man. This small book will go a long way in enabling us to know and understand the essential humanity of Bharathi, the poet.

Ka. Na. Subramaniam
"Have you read it?"
Swadesamitran
August 19, 1956

About the Translators

Premila Paul taught English Literature in the American College, Madurai for three decades and is currently the Director of SCILET (The Study Centre for Indian Literature in English and Translation) there. She taught Indian Literature and Women's Literature in the US for three years, and has published two books and articles on these subjects.

Subash Jeyan has a Ph.D in Tolkien and fantasy literature from CIEFL (currently EFLU), Hyderabad, and is a writer and editor, previously at *The Hindu Literary Review/Sunday Magazine* and presently at *Frontline*. He is also a birder, a long-distance endurance cyclist, a randonneur, a marathoner, and lives in Palakkad, Kerala.